AF292355

Ukrainian Humanism
Seven Essays on the Culture of a European Nation
by Giuseppe Antonio Perri

Sarmatica
© 2015 Riccardo Condò Editore
ISBN 9791280882028
Printed by Amazon kdp, U.S.A. under license of
Riccardo Condò Editore
Second edition
www.riccardocondoeditore.it
Riccardo Condò Editore, Pineto (Te), Italy

Giuseppe A. Perri

UKRAINIAN HUMANISM

*Seven Essays on the Culture
of a European Nation*

2022
Riccardo Condò Editore

In this volume I have gathered some of my writings, in English, French or Italian, presented at international Conferences, Seminars, Symposia etc., a part of which have appeared (or will appear), in amended form, in scholarly journals, collections of acts and proceedings of conferences.

As the title of the book indicates, each essay presents the figure of one of the main protagonists and builders of the multifaceted culture of Ukraine, which is one of the main expressions of European culture. Although often misunderstood or even imagined, by those who do not know it, as a provincial form of the wider "Russian" culture, the cultural life of Ukraine has always played, as will emerge from reading the following pages, the original and vital role of a transnational and transcultural hinge between different areas of the Slavic world and of the wider European world.

The essays collected here were all composed in the light of this cross-cultural inspiration, this being the key to understanding the history of this great country, for us so far and yet so close. After a brief introduction to the European and Latin nature of Ukrainian culture - the subject of my lecture at the historic hall of the Circle of Readers in Turin (hosted by the seventeenth century Palazzo Graneri della Roccia) - the reader will find an initial essay on the origins of the Cyrillic print culture. I presented this essay at the Seminar *Early Modern Print Culture in Central Europe* of the Academia Europaea, which was held in Wrocław (Poland) 16 to 18 September, 2013 (in a modified form it was published in the Proceedings of the Seminar by the Wrocław University Press). Then follows an essay on Skovoroda or the founder of the philosophy of Eastern Europe, in which his deep ties with the classical philosophies, which he learned at his *alma mater*, namely the Mohylian Academy of Kyïv, are reconstructed; the original theoretical synthesis produced by Skovoroda and its existential parable are also, in the same contribution, placed in parallel with the philosophical existence of Giordano Bruno; the essay is a version of my paper read at the Colloquium *Poetics of Selfhood: writing and other con-*

structions, Faculdade de Letras of the University of Lisbon, 3-5 March 2014 (an amended version of this paper should be published in the next issue - 2, 2015 - of *Kyiv-Mohyla Humanities Journal*, the international journal published by the National University of Kyiv-Mohyla Academy - NaUKMA).

The next essay presents the figure of Taras Ševčenko, the "father" of contemporary Ukrainian culture who, in the nineteenth century, established a Ukrainian poetic language and suffered the ordeal of a decade of forced recruitment in the Asian regions of the Russian Empire, with a ban imposed on him personally by the Tsar not to write or paint. Ševčenko was a servant (in the Russian Empire serfdom was not abolished until in 1861) whose artistic skills allowed him to enjoy the favor of some Russian Decembrist intellectuals who rescued him and allowed him to attend the Academy of Arts in St. Petersburg. The paper presents the role of Poland in the philosophy of history (perhaps the most influential literary genre in the Ukrainian cultural area) of the great poet and artist. I was asked to write this essay by the Ukrainian Section of the Inalco (Institut National des Langues et Civilisations Orientales) of Paris, a part of the University of Sorbonne Paris Cité; it will be published (in French) in the course of 2015 in the Proceedings of the study day in Paris dedicated in 2014 (the bicentenary of his birth) to Ševčenko.

There follows a work on the Polish-Ukrainian identity of the great writer Jarosław Iwaszkiewicz, whom I consider to be one of the best European writers. Seen as the last representative of the so-called "Ukrainian school" of Polish literature, Iwaszkiewicz was perhaps the most influential writer on the twentieth-century Polish art of fiction; his Ukrainian origins, in addition to being unquenchable stigmata on his personality and his work, are further evidence of the fruitfulness of the cross-cultural world of Ukraine. The work began as a contribution to the Conference *Borders*, organized by the Lincoln University of Pennsylvania (USA) in April of 2014 and was later published in the 2nd issue of *The Lincoln Humanities Journal*, in the autumn of 2014. "Independence: Literature, Historiography and Memory of the Ukrainian National Republic (1917-1921)" was conceived as a contribution to the *The First World War and Its Global Legacies: 100 Years On* (4-6 April 2014) organized by the Faculty of Education and Society at the University of Sunderland (UK), whose proceedings are being published. At the heart of the essay there are literary reactions, and memoirs about one of the major and most traumatic events of Ukrainian history, namely the collapse of Tsarism and the first proclamation of an independent Republic of Ukraine (January 1918). In addition to the memories of some of the protagonists and witnesses of those events, we review some literary repercussions in the works of Bulgakov (a Russian and Russian-speaking inhabitant of Kyïv) and Ukrainian authors like Stefanyk, Tyčyna, Chvyl'ovyj, etc.

The book ends with a short essay on the great Ukrainian novel *Shadows of forgotten ancestors* (*Tini zabutych predkiv*) by Mychajlo Kocjubyns'kyj, perhaps the greatest prose writer that Ukraine has ever had. The essay also examines the relationship between the novel (written in 1912) and the film version of 1964 made by the Soviet director of Armenian origin, Serhij Parajanov, and was the subject of my paper at the conference *Camera-Stylo: Intersections in Literature and Cinema* which was held at the University of Sydney (Australia), School of Letters, Art and Media, from 8 to April 10, 2015.

With this collection of essays I therefore offer a presentation of those who may be considered the "pillars" of modern Ukrainian culture, that is, those who have shaped the peculiar world view that is associated with this form of civilization, one of the most original and fruitful of the modern European world. Not surprisingly, these "pillars" include Iwaszkiewicz, a Polish-speaking author, since his literary work and his endless nostalgia for the Ukrainian plains vividly illustrate the eminently transcultural Ukrainian identity and, conversely, its strongly territorial anchor; a territory which Kostomarov, at the dawn of Ukrainian self-awareness in the first half of the nineteenth century, in his poem *Pisnja moja* (*My Song*, 1840) described in terms of a Ukraine, "which stretches from the San to the Sosna, touches the Carpathian clouds and bathes in the waters of the Black Sea."[1]

In the Appendix, the reader can find an essay of history of culture, which deals with a crucial period for the history of modern Ukraine: "*Korenizacija* as an ambiguous and temporary strategy of legitimization of Soviet power in Ukraine (1923-1933) and its legacy." In many

---

1 M.I. Kostomarov, *Tvory v dvoch tomach*, Kyïv 1990, p. 61. The San is the river that runs through Peremyšl' (the first city, now Polish, beyond the current Ukrainian-Polish border) while the Sosna (or Tycha Sosna) flows in the region of Belhorod, a city that now belongs to the Russian Federation and which is located just beyond the Russian-Ukrainian northern border.

regards, *korenizacija* is still considered a "golden age" of Ukrainian culture and language, but its ambiguity and tragic end are little known. The article appeared, in an amendend form, in *History of Communism in Europe*, 5, 2014.

In the acknowledgments, I would like to mention all the friends and colleagues who have shared with me the difficulties and intellectual joys that are contained in the following pages. My thanks, therefore, go first to Inna Skakovska who, with impassioned coaxing introduced me to the world of Ukrainian literature and history and has worked with me over the years of study that followed. Special thanks go to the members of Cierl (Centre Interdisciplinaire d'Étude des Religions et de la Laïcité) of the University of Brussels (ULB), especially the director, Anne Morelli, a leader of intellectual deconstruction. Next to her I would mention Cécile Vanderpelen-Diagre, whose encouragement helped me to continue with my researches, and Karine Alaverdian. I quote then all those with whom, as organizers or participants in international Symposia that have provided an opportunity for the preparation of most of the chapters of this book, I spoke in fruitful intellectual discussions, often prolonged in correspondence, of research, opinions, documentary and bibliographic references; namely: my dear friends Dominic Olariu, of the Department of Art History at the University of Marburg and Visiting Professor at the Max Planck Institute for the History of Science in Berlin, Jens Boysen, of the German Historical Institute in Warsaw and Professor at Lazarski University of Warsaw, and Lioudmila Chvedova of the Université de Lorraine, member and animator of the Cercle (Centre de Recherche sur les Cultures et les Littératures Européennes); then, Paulo Jesus and Gonçalo Marcelo of the Faculty of Arts, University of Lisbon, Olga Poliukhovych, together with the editorial board of *Kyiv-Mohyla Humanities Journal*. A special mention must be reserved for Irina Dmytrychyn, of the Inalco of Paris, the competent and impassioned leader of the Ukrainian Section, and to all the members of that organization, with whom it was so enjoyable to work for the organization of the *Journée houtsule* (March, 23, 2015). Worthy of mention are also the kindness and depth of thought of Abbes Maazaoui, of Lincoln University of Pennsylvania, Dimitrios Petrogiannis, University of Sunderland, Tim Grady of the University of Chester and Peter Marks of the University of Sydney.

Sincere and special thanks go to Aude Merlin, ULB professor and specialist of the Caucasian world, for the rich cultural exchanges and for the interest and appreciation that she has always shown for my work, and Ludwika (Ludka, in the poem that Iwaszkiewicz dedicated to her) Włodek, who, with patient friendship, answered all my questions about Jarosław. I also thank, warmly, the Skovorodian scholar, who needs no introduction, Stephen Scherer (of Central Michigan University) for his help and for the documentation he provided me; the same goes for Natalia Pylypiuk (University of Alberta) and Maria Grazia Bertolini (University of Milan), who, with extraordinary kindness, have provided me with information and documentation on their Skovorodian works, of great importance for me.

The frequent exchanges of ideas with Olivier Dupuis (long-time European MP and secretary of the Nonviolent Radical Party, Transnational and Transparty), along with his passionate, sincere and educated political vocation, were for me a constant reference point in the analysis of the current difficult situation in Ukraine. I am also grateful to Italian friends Silvja Manzi and Igor Boni, of the Adelaide Aglietta Association of Turin, for organizing the beautiful presentation of the Italian transaltion of Kocjubyns'kyj's novel at the Circle of Readers of Turin, and to the architect Renzo Boatelli (who divides his time between Italy and Ukraine), for the exchange of opinions and true, precious friendship that he has always reserved for me, and the artistic couple Tetiana Kuzina and Aliano Frediani, whose piano playing gave me moral support during these labors. A primary role was played in my research work by the fruitful editorial collaboration that I had with Stefano Rolle and Stefania Iannizzotto (Fellow of the Accademia della Crusca); the lucky reencounter of a dear childhood friend, the enlightened publisher Riccardo Condò, then made possible the publication of this book. An invaluable helping hand in the collection of a part of the documentation was given by Inna Poljanovs'ka and Pavel Kozlov, as was the revision of the English manuscript by Barbara Elizabeth Lewis. All contents and any possible errors contained in the book are, of course, of my making and are my exclusive responsibility.

Brussels, Belgium
January 2016

Author's Note on Nomenclature, Transliteration and Translations

The scientific system (IST, International Scholarly Transliteration) of transliteration from Cyrillic is employed in the volume. For Ukrainian names and place names I have transliterated directly from Ukrainian. All translations are mine.

A table of equivalents in the Library of Congress (LC) system
is given below.
Ukrainian alphabet

Cyrillic	IST	LC
А	a	a
Б	b	b
В	v	v
Г	h	h
Ґ	g	g
Д	d	d
Е	e	e
Є	je	ie
Ж	ž	zh
З	z	z
И	y	y
І	i	i
Ї	ï (ji)	Ï (i is used more often)
Й	j	Ï (i is used more often)
К	к	k
Л	l	l
М	m	m
Н	n	n
О	o	o
П	p	p
Р	r	r
С	s	Ss
Т	t	t
У	u	Uu
Ф	f	f
Х	ch (x)	kh
Ц	c	ts
Ч	č	ch
Ш	š	sh
Щ	šč	shch
ь	’	’ (is usually omitted)
Ю	ju	iu
Я	ja	ia
’	”	(omitted)

1. LATIN UKRAINE

Lecture held October 10, 2014 at the Circle of Readers of Turin

If it is true, as has often been argued, that Russian history (which inevitably ends up being mentioned when talking about Ukraine) has swung constantly over the centuries between Europe and Asia, the same cannot be said for Ukraine, which is instead an entirely European land. For many reasons, Ukrainian identity is fully European; from a geographic point of view, this is easy to understand but unfortunately underestimated by many; for example, in terms of purely spatial distance, Kyïv (Kiev in Russian, Kijów in Polish) is almost the same distance from Trieste as Trieste is from Palermo, Sicily. And as regards Italy and other European nations, a part of the national territory lived with Western Ukraine for nearly two centuries in the same national community (the former Habsburg Empire), resulting in a mixing and mingling which, however, is rarely discussed. However, Ukraine should be considered truly European, especially for the fact that it belonged in the modern era to the Polish-Lithuanian Rzeczpospolita which, in the sixteenth and seventeenth centuries, was the largest European state and was considered, by the other Western states, to be a fully continental entity. The concept (of Enlightenment and eighteenth-century origin) of Eastern Europe or Central-Eastern Europe did not yet exist and Poland was considered part of Western Europe or, better, "Latin" Europe. Poland defined itself as *antemurale Christianitatis* ("rampart of Christendom"), i.e. the extreme border of the Catholic or Latin Christendom.

Ukraine, in its generating phase, i.e. in the early modern period, when the Ukrainian people as such was born, and all the peoples of Europe came into existence, was imbued with this Latinness, which was derived from living, wholly, inside the Polish state. This despite the fact that Ukraine was an Orthodox land. But we must take into account that *Slavia orthodoxa*, and especially Ukraine, is very different from what is imagined: first, it was only partially "Graecised" from the beginning and then, especially in the period we are examining, was permeated by the Latin culture, above all through the school system that the Jesuits instituted in the Polish-Lithuanian Commonwealth, setting up schools, colleges and universities based on their famous *ratio studiorum*. This phenomenon of Latin Jesuit schooling, which attached great importance to the classical past (especially Latin) and was innervated by Italian and European Humanistic-Renaissance culture, strongly influenced Polish and Ukrainian cultural life; consider, for example, that many Polish kings used Italian as the language of communication at court, also for the presence in Poland of Italian nobles and wealthy merchants and of Queen Bona Sforza.

Ukrainian Orthodoxy therefore came into contact with this expansion of Latin culture at the hands of the Polish Commonwealth and imitated the Jesuit system of study, taking it as a model for the establishment in Ukraine, as of the end of the sixteenth century, of important study centers based on humanistic training and pedagogy. The most important of these centers is what was then called the Academy of Kyïv, founded in 1632 by the Metropolitan Petro Mohyla, who was also very close to the Polish authorities. Mohyla also promoted the acquisition of a considerable number of books published in the West (in Venice, Amsterdam, etc.), translations and local publications, which over time made the collection of books in the possession of the Academy consistent. The courses of the Mohylian College were held in Latin and the students carried out compulsory exercises of versification in Latin: all the students had to write poems in Latin; Cicero, Sallust and Ovid were among the authors most beloved among the teachers and students of the Academy, which produced, in turn, important cultural personalities.

Seventeenth-century Kyïv belonged then to Western Europe, as Poland was truly European; certainly, Ukraine was the real physical rampart of Western Europe, that is, that "wild" area, to colonize and civilize but in a material sense: *Dyke Pole* or wild lands were the name given to the uninhabited steppes that served as the border between Ukraine, the Tatar Crimea and Muscovy, which had instead lived until recently in the direct sphere of Mongolian influence. Although Muscovites had shaken off during the fifteenth century what Russian historians call the Mongol "yoke", they did not participate in this phenomenon of Latinization of culture that spread in the sixteenth and seventeenth centuries to Central-Eastern Europe. Ukraine's position also favored an important flow of exchanges and relations with the Tatar, Islamic and Ottoman world. So Ukraine belonged to Western Europe for the entire duration of Early modernity.

Subsequently, from the historical point of view, there was the great national anti-Polish uprising of 1648, led by the Cossack hetman Bohdan Chmel'nyc'kyj (whose statue, built in the nineteenth century by Tsar Nicholas I, is placed today in the high city of Kyïv) which led to the birth of a Ukrainian Cossack state (Hetmanate) independent of the Polish Rzeczpospolita and federated to the Muscovite kingdom. The Hetmanate remained autonomous for about 150 years and was later incorporated into the Russian Empire, falling within its province at the end of the eighteenth century. The Hetmanate occupied Central-Eastern Ukraine, from Kyïv and Dnieper (Dnipro in Ukrainian) to the Muscovy. Then, during the partitions of Poland in the late eighteenth century, the Muscovite state, called the Russian Empire by Peter the Great, also took possession of the Right Bank of the Dnipro (west-central Ukraine), but not Galicia, which is that part of Ukraine which has never belonged to the Russian Empire or the Russian statehood of any kind. This until 1939 when, as a result of the infamous Hitler-Stalin Pact, the Soviet Union occupied Galicia and the city of L'viv (Lvov), immediately deporting a million people from that area and thus contributing to an anti-Soviet hostility that was reflected in the spread of the armed movement (Upa, Ukrainian Insurgent Army) led by Stepan Bandera. After an initial collaboration with the Germans, Upa turned to fight Soviets, Germans and Poles, giving rise to one of the most controversial and painful phases of the recent history of Ukraine.

What is important to emphasize here is that a part of Ukraine has never been part of the Russian Empire and thus retained its own strong identity; in general, however, it can be said that the period of approximately 120 years that run between the end of the eighteenth century and the Russian Revolution, did not allow the denationalization and de-Latinization of the part of Ukraine which was submitted to the Russian imperial government. One should consider this point carefully, because this time-span is the same as that which enabled Poland to emerge almost intact after the First World War and to rebuild its nation state, which is basically what happened in Ukraine when a Ukrainian People's Republic was formed in 1917, and declared independence in January 1918. The Bolsheviks, as we know, did not recognize this independence and waged war on the Republic of Ukraine; but Soviet power had then to recognize the existence of an Ukrainian entity, unlike the Tsarist state that tended not to accept the existence of a cultural, national and political Ukrainian autonomy, preferring to use the name of Little Russia; we know that even in the second half of the nineteenth century it took at least two imperial decrees to ban the use of the Ukrainian language.

In 1921, Ukraine became one of the Soviet Union Republics, with the right to secession, which was largely theoretical for a long time, but was eventually exercised in 1991 to legally give life to the current independent state of Ukraine. Moreover, in the first ten years of Soviet life an important, albeit ambiguous, policy of enhancement of national cultures or *korenizacija* ("indigenization") was enforced and therefore also of Ukrainian culture; this enabled Ukranians to make important strides in the rediscovery and enhancement of their national past, of the Latin and European Ukraine.

And this is why, in 1991, an entity that was obscure to the superficial glance of those who had lived on this side of the so-called Iron Curtain re-emerged once again, but it had always been there and had also had an important role, because it was the Ukrainians who westernized and "Europeanized" Russia for the first time, when Moscow seized the Ukrainian regions of the Polish-Lithuanian state. This first phase of westernization of Russia was followed by a second round of direct access to Western sources promoted by Peter the Great, and finally produced the great age of nineteenth-century Russian literature and culture. But the beginning of this cultural flowering was handled by clerics of the Ukrainian Academy of Kyïv, who were called, even by Peter the Great, in mass to Russia to occupy Episcopal sees and constitute Academies and centers of study. The most important exponent of this academic kyïvian culture was the great philosopher Hryhorij Skovoroda, translator of Ovid, Cicero and Plutarch, author of many important philosophical dialogues, with a distinct personality, which has often led critics to rightly compare him to Socrates or St. Francis of Assisi. Although he lived a retiring existence and did not publish anything in the course of his life, Skovoroda is considered the founder of the autonomous philosophy of *Slavia orthodoxa*.

Even Gogol', a great author who wrote in Russian and one of the protagonists of the Golden Age of Russian literature, was Ukrainian; he was indeed a great expert on Ukrainian history, so that for a certain period of his life he had thought of a career as a historian of Ukraine; not surprisingly, *Taras Bul'ba* begins with the return home from the Kyïv Academy of the two young sons of Taras, who had studied there before returning to the house on the steppe. There are also other personalities that one does not imagine as having originated from this Ukrainian-Polish melting pot, such as Dostoevskij, whose last name is clearly of Ukrainian-Polish origin. Although his son revealed in certain passages of his novels that he entertained some form of anti-Polish sentiment, Dostoevskij's father had attended the theological college of Kam"janec'-Podil's'kyj, then capital of Podolia (in Central-Western Ukraine) and subsequently emigrated to Russia.

In short, contrary to common belief, i.e. that Ukraine is nothing but a sort of offshoot of Russian culture, we may affirm, on the basis of the above, that there are trends which reveal exactly the opposite.

From the literary point of view, the vernacular Slavic Europe literatures were all born slightly later than those of Western Europe: Polish literature had its beginnings in the sixteenth and seventeenth centuries, Russian at the end of the eighteenth century, and also Ukrainian literature, because previously there was the fierce competition of Church Slavonic, Polish and Latin (which was the official language of the Polish-Lithuanian Commonwealth). Ukrainian literature came into existence precisely when Ukrainian language and culture were really put in danger as a result of the Russian conquest; the founder of Ukrainian literature is Ivan Kotljarevs'kyj, from the same region as Gogol' (the area of Poltava, in Central-Eastern Ukraine), who wrote the first poem in vernacular Ukrainian: *Eneïda*, a paraphrase with a grotesque tone of Virgil's poem, set among the Cossacks. Then in the nineteenth century there was the great poet considered the father of the Ukrainian language and literature, still much revered in Ukraine, Taras Ševčenko. Finally, at the end of the nineteenth century, there was a great flourishing, modern and European, of Ukrainian literature, with authors of great depth, such as Kocjubyns'kyj, Lesja Ukraïnka, Ol'ha Kobyljans'ka, Stefanyk; their works have been translated into French, English and German. The most "European" of these authors was perhaps Mychajlo Kocjubyns'kyj, who also said in some of his letters that he preferred non-Slavic literatures to Slavic and introduced into Ukrainian literature themes of Scandinavian symbolism and the decadentism of continental Modernism.

During the Soviet regime, the European preferences of Ukrainian intellectuals reemerged in the second half of the Twenties with the writer Mykola Chvyl'ovyj, but he met with Stalin's personal excommunication. The following decade was terrible for Ukrainian culture, being as it was one of the main targets of Stalin's purges. Even the long postwar stagnation had produced negative effects on Ukrainian cultural identity, forcing more and more forms of provincialisation and Russification, but this trend was interrupted in the Sixties by the blossoming of a generation of young militant intellectuals. These same people gathered to guide the movement for human rights in last years of the Soviet Union and also tried, unsuccessfully, to guide the governments in the early decades of the newfound independence; the governments remained firmly in the hands of the economic-financial oligarchy, largely coming from the ranks of the former communist nomenclature.

The political and cultural battle for Europe is still ongoing in Ukraine and it is no coincidence that the protest movement born at the end of 2013 has as its reference point the attempt to anchor Ukraine to the destiny of the European Union. The intellectuals and writers of the new Ukraine are at the forefront in this challenge, even those of the Russian language such as Andrej Kurkov, along with Lina Kostenko, Oksana Zabužko, Jurij Andruchovyč, Maria Matios, Oleksandr Myched, and many others.

2. Print Culture in Early Modern Ukraine

Paper presented at the Seminar: "Early Modern Print Culture in Central Europe" of the Academia Europaea, held in Wrocław 16 to 18 September 2013; in a modified form it is now contained in the Proceedings of the Seminar, edited by Stefan Kiedron and Anna-Maria Rimm, Wrocław 2015

1. Ukraine was, and still is, a borderland, between East and West, Latin and Byzantine worlds, Christianity and Islam. In the early modern age the function of mediation among different civilizations was intrinsic to Ukraine as it belonged to the Kingdom of Poland and to the Lithuanian-Ruthenian Grand Duchy (and, after 1569, to the *Rzeczpospolita* - Polish-Lithuanian Commonwealth). With the progressive absorption of Ukraine into the Muscovite Kingdom (after the Chmel'nyc'kyj Uprising of 1648) its identity and importance as a crossroad of civilizations were obscured. The awareness of a distinct Ukrainian identity within the Russian Empire was been kept alive, throughout the XVII and XVIII centuries, by the Cossack nobility who enjoyed a wide autonomy in the government of the Western provinces of the Empire (Hetmanate). But the dismantling of the Hetmanate by the Tsars at the end of the XVIII century weakened this identity; an anonymous text of the early XIX century, *Istorija Rusov* [*History of the Rus*], collecting the facts narrated by the Cossack chronicles, reserved as a cornerstone and a source of XIX-century Ukrainian national pride[1]. Both Nikolaj Gogol' (1809-1852) - who was Ukrainian, and who, with his Taras Bul'ba (1834), greatly contributed to the knowledge of the Ukrainian world in Russia and in Europe - and Taras Ševčenko (1814-1861), the Ukrainian nation-

---

1 Rus' (not to be confused with "Russia") was the name of the first East Slavic state, born around the city of Kyïv (IX century) often used by early modern Ukrainians to indicate their territories.

al poet, drew from *Istorija Rusov* amongst their sources. In the second half of the XIX century the movement "Ukrainophilia" generated, in Tsarist Ukraine, a wave of nation building and scientific study of the Ukrainian past. Volodymyr Antonovyč a leading exponent of the Ukrainophilia, headed the Imperial commission that compiled and published the voluminous *Archiv Jugo-Zapadnoj Rossii* [*Archives of Southwestern Russia*][2], still the main source for the history of Ukraine.

In 1904 Mychajlo Hruševs'kyj, a former student of Antonovyč, wrote a revolutionary brief essay, published in the collection of Russian Academy of Sciences, in which he challenged the imperial narrative of the history of the East Slavs and the traditional scheme of Russian history, commencing the construction of the Ukrainian national paradigm[3]. Twenty years later, Ivan Ohijenko wrote the first history of Ukrainian printing[4].

2. As early as in 1740, one of the first bibliologists, Johann Daniel Hoffmann, cited Ukrainian printing in L'viv, Ostroh, and Kyïv and some of their publications[5]. The first scientific work on the history of Western Ukrainian printing was a text - in Polish - by Denys Zubryc'kyj, a Galician Russophile who gained access to archival material of the L'viv Brotherhood[6]. In 1850, the rector of the Russian Saint Vladimir University in Kyïv, Mychajlo Maksymovyč, made the first attempt – in Russian - to study the history of early printing in the entire Ukraine, based on surveys he carried out in old libraries of Central Ukraine[7]. A noteworthy book in Russian was authored by Ivan Karataev (1883), who accurately described many ancient Cyrillic incunabula[8]. In his Russian book (1918) Fedor Titov, professor of theology at the Kyïvian Academy[9], discussed the printing activity of the Kyïvian Monastery of the Caves (Kyïv Pečers'ka Lavra), which began in the XVII century. The Russian studies shared an all-Russian narrative assumption and failed to distinguish an autonomous

---

2 Southwestern Russia and Little Russia were the names used in XIX-century Russian Empire to designate Ukraine.
3 For an English translation: Hruševs'kyj 1988.
4 Ohijenko 1994.
5 Hoffmann 1740.
6 Zubrzycki 1836.
7 Maksimovič 1880, pp. 661-716.
8 Karataev 1883.
9 Titov 1918.

Ukrainian cultural world. Among many Polish studies about early modern printing in Poland and Gran Duchy of Lithuania, published before Ohijenko's book, particularly noteworthy is Johannes Ptasnik's work about early printing in Cracow, which presents, inter alia, 50 documents about Schweipolt Fiol (1460?-1525-6), who is the first printer of Cyrillic books[10].

Then, before World War I there were only very few studies about Ukrainian printing written in Ukrainian and from a Ukrainian point of view. Ivan Ohijenko was one of the assistants of Professor Volodymyr Peretc, a prominent Ukrainian literary historian and bibliologist, who set up in the University of Kyïv – in wartime - a team of researchers on the history of Ukrainian printing; in particular, Ohijenko developed a method for establishing the dating publications, based on the analysis of font design[11]. He left Ukraine after the war, but his colleague Serhij Maslov, taking advantage of the favorable climate for Ukrainian culture typical of the first decade of the Soviet rule, founded the Ukraïns'kyj Naukovyj Instytut Knyhoznavstva (Ukrainian Scientific Institute of Bibliology)[12] in 1922 and, in 1924, published *Drukarstvo na Ukraïni v XVI—XVIII st.*[13], a small but accurate work based on the regional grouping (Galicia, Volhynia, Kyïv, Černihiv) of printing activities; although archival materials used in the study had already been published, it was the first reliable overview of printing materials about Ukrainian Cyrillic print.

3. The following year, Ohijenko published in L'viv the first of a planned 8-volume history of Ukrainian books: I. Ohijenko, *Istorija Ukraïns'koho Drukarstva [A History of Ukrainian Printing]*, L'viv, 1925, 388 pages; the book was condemned by the Soviet regime and reprinted in Ukraine only in 1994 (except a reprint by the Ukrainian diaspora, in Winnipeg in 1983). This first volume was conceived as a survey of the sources and of the printed literature; its subtitle was: "Historical and bibliographical review of Ukrainian publishing - XV-XVII centuries." However, Ohijenko not only wrote about the sources and analyzed the views of his predecessors, but also gave a

---

10 Ptasnik 1922.
11 Isajevyč 2002, p. 21.
12 The Institute was close down in the 1930's, when Stalin decided to destroy the Ukrainian intelligentsia.
13 Maslov 1924.

brief outline of printers and their employees, following the order of Maslov's regions. He supplied some material about the Polish, Russian and Hebrew printing in Ukraine, as well. Indeed, with his *Istorija Ukraïns'koho Drukarstva*, Ohijenko produced the first history of Ukrainian printing. The materials compiled for the other volumes are preserved in Ohijenko's archives (now at S. Andrew's College in Winnipeg); however, much of the scholar's archives burned in Lublin in 1944[14].

For more than six decades, Ohijenko's work was held in the Soviet *specschovy* (hidden) Libraries Department, remaining practically inaccessible even to experts. In fact, the Ukrainian studies suffered a lot in Soviet times, particularly from the 1930s on, when Stalin decided to put the Russian nationalist ideology at the core of the Soviet identity[15]. It was only 2002 that a text of real scientific value came out: Jaroslav Isajevyč, *Ukraïns'ke Knyhovydannja: vytoky, rozvytok, problemy* [*The Ukrainian Publishing; Origins, Development, Problems*] was published in L'viv by Instytut Ukraïnoznavstva I. Kryp'jakevyča and has since come to be the reference text in the field. In the international literature, the only text of note that deals with the Ukrainian printing, was authored by Lubomyr R. Wynar (a representative of the Ukrainian diaspora in Northern America) and published in Denver in 1962 as part of the Colorado University Studies in Librarianship, although a note of the editor unexpected affirmed that it was "a fine study [...], though of limited interest"[16].

4. In his study, Ohijenko states that the first Cyrillic printed book appeared in Cracow in 1491[17], two years before a book printed in Obod-Cetinje in Montenegro, that some scholar, such as Tomanovič, had presented as the first Cyrillic printed book[18]. A book issued in Venice in 1483, was the first one printed in Glagolitic characters; it targeted Croatian readers only because these characters were not popular with East Slavic nations.

---

14 Isajevyč 2002, p. 26. In 1940, Ohijenko was tonsured, assumed the monastic name of Ilarion and was ordained as the orthodox Bishop of Chełm (Cholm); in 1944 he became the Metropolite of Chełm and Lublin. In 1947, he settled down in Winnipeg, where he soon became the Metropolitan bishop of the Ukrainian Orthodox Church of Canada.
15 Brandenberger 2002.
16 Baillie 1962, p. III.
17 Ohijenko 1994, p. 35.
18 Tomanovič 1900, p. 431.

The two books printed in Cracow in 1491 were in the Church Slavonic language with a Ukrainian "tinge" (as stated by Ohijenko and Wynar): *Časoslov* [*The Book of Hours*][19] and an *Oktoich* [*Octoechos*, i.e. a liturgical Orthodox book that contains canons and religious hymns].[20] The printer was Schweipolt Fiol, a German from Neustadt in Franconia, who like many other Germans emigrated to Poland, where Polish kings very readily welcomed skilled artisans. Initially involved in the mining industry, Fiol may have learned the Ruthenian tongue in Lublin. Another German resident of Cracow, Rudolf Borsdorf, prepared the Cyrillic letters following Fiol's instructions[21]. There has been much speculation about who the patron of Fiol's work was; according to Wynar, the only valid explanation is that "Fiol was printing at the request of some prominent priests of the Ukrainian Orthodox Church"[22]. Isajevyč supports this hypothesis corroborated by the fact that in both colophons - of *Časoslov* and *Oktoich* - Fiol emphasized his German origin. Isajevyč explains that

the true - Orthodox - initiators would prefer to remain in the shadows, knowing that the German Catholic was the least suspected of wanting to issue books to the detriment of the Catholic faith. The mention that the printer is of "German family" was probably intended to create an impression that printing was only business, and disguise the real motives of the organizers. Despite these precautions, clouds gathered over printing in Ciryllic. In November 1491 Fiol was imprisoned as a heretic. Shortly after his release from prison, he was forced into Levoča (Eastern Slovakia)[23].

Isajevyč supposes, too, that the orthodox eparchy of Peremyšl' (Polish Przemyśl), close to Cracow and with an intense cultural life, was involved in Fiol's printing. An important role was also played by Jan Turzo, who was the owner of the mines where Fiol worked as a technician and who financed his printing business in Cyrillic. According to Karen Lambrecht, the rich and powerful Hungarian Turzo family, with their international profile and their network of allies and friends, had a remarkable role in facilitating intercultural communi-

---

19 Copies are available in the "Vernads'kyj" National Library of Ukraine, Kyïv (NLVUK) and the Moscow state Library (MSL).
20 A copy is available in MSL.
21 Ohijenko 1994, p. 41.
22 Wynar 1962, p. 21.
23 Isajevyč 2002, pp. 90-91.

cations in Early Modern Central Europe[24]. Jan Turzo later became the Archibishop of Wrocław (1506-1520).

Given Fiol's Ruthenian and Orthodox clientele from Ukraine as well as his use, in Cyrillic letters, of Church Slavonic with a Ukrainian "tinge", the prominent Ukrainian historians of Ukrainian printing open their works with discussions of the books printed by Fiol. It is, indeed, an acceptable historiographic choice, be it for no other reason that a wide circulation of Fiol's books among Ukrainian readers; but we must not forget the international character of the Fiol enterprise, implemented in Poland, by a German craftsman funded by a Hungarian entrepreneur.

Fiol's *Oktoich* consists of 169 printed leaves in folio without printed numerals, with 25 or 26 lines per page. Časoslov consists of 769 pages. They had only scant decoration and used 230 different letters. Fiol's incunabula had many imperfections: his type was clearly cut but dense in spacing, and the margins in many places were irregular[25]. Fiol published three more undated books: a *Triod' cvetnaja* [*Pentecostarion* or *Flowery Triodion*][26], a *Triod' postnaja* [*Fasting Triodion*][27] and a book of Psalms, which has been lost. Fiol's publications circulated widely across Ukraine, Belarus and other Orthodox countries. In Russia, where the first copy was imported in 1517, they were long used, especially among Old Believer communities. Today we know that 126 copies (identified or described) may have survived[28], 9 of which are *Oktoich* (with only one of them complete, once preserved in in the library of St. Elisabeth's Church in Wrocław and now kept in the Russian State Library of Moscow). A copy of *Triod' cvetnaja* is kept in the New York Public Library.

5. The second printing enterprise analyzed in the main Ukrainian historical reconstructions of print culture in early Modern Ukraine (Ohijenko, Wynar, Isajevyč), is that run by Franciscus Skoryna (before 1490-ca. 1551), a scholar that was born in Polack, a town which belonged to the Lithuanian Grand Duchy (now to northern Belarus).

---

24 Lambrecht 1998.
25 Wynar 1962, pp. 24-26.
26 Copies are available in the MSL and Biblioteka Narodowa [National Library], Warszawa (BNW).
27 Copies are available in the NLVUK, the MSL and the BNW.
28 Wynar 1962, p. 27.

The Lithuanian Grand Duchy was a multinational state with a social and cultural cooperation between the Lithuanian rulers and the Slavic people; actually, Ukrainians and Belarusians shared religion, culture and a common language, i.e. Ruthenian (the old Rus' language, with local nuances). As Skoryna's vernacular printed language was closer to the Belarusian variant of the Ruthenian language, he is currently considered one of the fathers of the Belarusian language. Therefore Skoryna should in fact be ranked as an epitome of Ruthenian-Belarusian print culture. He is included in the histories of Ukrainian printing because Ruthenian culture is the common source of the Ukrainian and the Belarusian ones, and because his books circulated largely in Ukraine.

Skoryna was born into a wealthy merchant family and graduated from Universities in Cracow and Padua (1512). Skoryna chose Prague as most favorable place for publishing Cyrillic books, where the Hussite movement had prompted an unprecedented rise of cultural and political life. The first translation of the Bible into one of the Slavic languages was published, not incidentally, in Prague. On 6 August, 1517, Skoryna's *Psaltyr'* [*Psalter*][29] was published in Church Slavonic with annotations in the vernacular language. The publisher pointed out that the book can be used "by children as the beginning of all good learning." The book consisting of 142 leaves, in a convenient format (quarto). Skoryna's real aim was to translate the Bible into Ruthenian; therefore, he published 22 separated Bible books over the next two years[30]. The printing was supported, as Ohijenko points out, by Bohdan Onkov, a rich merchant of Vilnius.[31] In 1525 Skoryna transferred his press from Prague to Vilnius, where he issued *Apostol* [*The Acts of the Apostles*][32], but soon he had to stop his printing activity because of serious personal and financial troubles[33]. According to Ohijenko, Skoryna asked some German masters to prepare the Cyrillic letters[34].

All Ukrainian scholars emphasize the high level of Skoryna's printing; Isajevyč's opinion is that, "although Prague was the center of an-

---

29 A copy is available in the MSL.
30 Copies of 22 books are available in the MSL; of 9 books in the NLVUK.
31 Ohijenko 1994, p. 49.
32 A copy is available in the MSL.
33 Wynar 1962, p. 35.
34 Ohijenko 1994, p. 49.

cient printing, at that time there was no Czech editions of such highly artistic Renaissance design, as in the printing of Frančišak Skoryna"[35]. For Wynar, "it is necessary to emphasize the high degree of technological excellence of his printing"[36]. Skoryna introduced a title page in Slavic incunabula and did not imitated (unlike Fiol) the features of manuscript books. His books are richly decorated with woodcuts, engravings, ornamental initials (like contemporaneous Italian and German books) and also portraits of the publisher, an unprecedented detail never seen afterwards. Skoryna was inspired by humanistic ideals, and his translations were marked by a desire to make them understandable to "simple people." Hence, he used many grammatical and lexical "belarusianisms." On account of this, Ivan Franko, a prominent Ukrainian writer, defined Skoryna's printing not only as a literary fact, but also as an important contribution to the history of culture. Interestingly, there are numerous handwritten copies of the Bible and Skoryna's other printed texts[37].

6. Ruthenian-Belarusian was also the beginning, in the early 1560s in Nesviž (a village owned by Prince Mikołaj Radziwiłł), of the printed books used to disseminate religious ideas, in this case Protestant ones. It was in Nesviž in 1562 that the Calvinist Semeon Budnyj (1530-1593), aided by the pastor Lavrentij Kryškovs'kij, published *Katechyzys* [*Catechism*][38], which consisted of 256 leaves. Because the type used in the Nesviž press was very close to Skoryna's type, Ohijenko suggest that Skoryna's equipment was handed over to them. The prince's death in 1565 and his son reconversion to Catholicism put an end to the Nesviž Calvinist printing[39]. Patriotic and religious aims inspired the printing ventures of the Belarusian Protestant Vasyl' Tjapyns'kyj (Polish Wasyl Ciapiński), the first Slavic wandering printer, who published *Evanhelie* [*The Gospel*] in the early 1570s, without engraved illustrations except the ornamental initial letters and with the type similar to that used by Skoryna and Budnyj. At the time of publication, this Gospel was unique in that it featured the Church Slavonic text and a translation into the language of "simple folk" (that

---

35 Isajevyč 2002, p. 96.
36 Wynar 1962, pp. 36-37.
37 Isajevyč 2002, pp. 99-100.
38 A copy is available in the MSL.
39 Ohijenko 1994, p. 57.

is, Belarusians and Ukrainians) next to each other. Tjapyns'kyj provided also etymological explanations of words and passages. These materials demonstrate that he had a good knowledge of science and philology[40]. In his didactic, Protestant–inflected *Foreword* to the Gospel, Tjapyns'kyj, articulated the stereotypical of the abandonment of Ruthenian identity after the Union of Lublin, which was to find its almost famous expression in the *Threnos* (1610) of the prominent orthodox writer Meletij Smotryc'kyj (ca.1577-1633), who later converted and joined the Uniate Church. The Gospel of Tjapyns'kyj has been preserved only in two copies, one of wich is kept in the Regional Museum of Archangel'sk (Russia).

7. Finally, the first Ukrainian book actually printed in Ukraine was published in L'viv, by a Muscovite craftsman. The press founder was, in fact, a refugee from Moscow, Ivan Fedorov (ca. 1520-1583), who arrived in Vilnius in 1566 with his collaborator Pëtr Mstislavec. Two years before, they had printed *Apostol* in Moscow, but the Russian clergy – as Fedorov affirmed in the *Colophon* of his L'viv *Apostol* (1574)[41] - were hostile to printed books and forced them to leave Moscow. In Vilnius, they were invited by the prominent nobleman Hryhorij Chodkevyč to establish a printing house in Zabludiv (Podlasie). Here they printed *Evanhelie Učitel'noe* [*The Instructive Gospel*] (399 leaves in folio) in 1568[42]. Based on the similarity of the types used in Zabludiv and in Moscow, Maslov supposed that Fedorov had an opportunity to bring the printing equipment in from Russia[43]. In 1573 he was in L'viv: he could learn about the cultural and educational activities of the L'viv middle classes. That is why he hoped that in L'viv he could find favorable conditions for self-publishing. Some indications hint at printing activity in L'viv predating Ivan Fedorov's arrival there, but no such books have been preserved.

All the illuminations of the L'viv *Apostol* (15 plus 264 leaves in folio) are ornamental plants, and the book has a high artistic value. Compared to the work made in Moscow, Fedorov used orthographic variants which were in use in Ukraine. But the emphasis was mostly the same as in Moscow *Apostol*; according to Isajevyč, isolated cases

---

40 Isajevyč 2002, p. 103.
41 Copies are available in the NLVUK and the MSL.
42 Copies are available in NLVUK and MSL.
43 Maslov 1924, p. 32.

of the Ukrainian accent type suggest that Ukrainian assemblers were involved in production[44]. One copy of this book is to be found in the New York Public Library, and another one in the Harvard University Library (Harvard hosts one of the most important centres of the Ukrainian studies); a handful copies are preserved in L'viv and Kyïv libraries.

In 1836 Denys Zubryc'kyj expressed his belief that there had to be other books printed in L'viv by Fedorov. But the scientists and the public became aware only in 1954 of the existence of another print – an *Azbuka* (*Primer*) published in L'viv in 1574 - through an article of Roman Jakobson[45]. The discovered copy now is in the Library of the Harvard University. In 1984 there was a report on another copy, acquired by the London British Library. This *Primer* is the first textbook in Ukrainian. According to Isajevyč,

it was associated with the educational plans for the Ukrainian middle class, who gradually raised the level of their schools. In 1572 representatives of "the whole Rus' community and the burghers" of L'viv made a petition to the Royal power concerning the recognition of their right to send children to schools and to study "liberal arts" and in April 1575 they achieved the support of this resolution. The publication of the *Primer* has contributed to the implementation of the program of educational activities[46].

In 1575 Fedorov left L'viv for Ostroh, in Volhynia; here, *knjaz'* (prince) Kostjantyn Ostroz'kyj had founded an Academy and initiated the project of translating and print the entire Bible in Church Slavonic. This ambitious project lasted five years and involved the best personalities of the Orthodox culture. Finally, in 1581, Fedorov printed the famous *Ostrohian Bible* (628 leaves of petit type in folio)[47], one of the most important literary monument in Eastern Europe; the first 5 pages, not numbered, contained the title, the coat of arms of Ostroz'kyj and two preface in Greek and Church Slavonic by the *knjaz'* and Herasym Smotryc'kyj, who led the commission of translators. The wealth of Ostroz'kyj and the expertise of Fedorov produced an excellent work[48], printed in black and red, with orna-

---

44 Isajevyč 2002, p. 113.
45 Jakobson 1955.
46 Isajevyč 2002, p. 117.
47 Copies are available in NLVUK and MSL.
48 Maslov 1924, p. 40.

ments (flower designs, engraved initials, and capital letters). In 1582 Fedorov returned in L'viv, but the Ostroh press continued to print, issuing several publications. All of them were devised to defend the Orthodox faith; one of the most famous Ostroh's issues was *Apokrysys* by Chrystofor Filalet (1598)[49]. With the death, in 1608, of the *knjaz'* Kostjantyn, his son decided to embrace Catholicism; consequently, both the Academy and printing practically ceased in Ostroh.

All in all, there are 28 specimens of Ostroh printing registered throughout its lifetime. Of these, only seven are liturgical. Other texts include mainly manuals, theological works and anti-Catholic, anti-Uniate and partly anti-Protestant *pamphlets* (10 publications). As for languages, Ostroh's printings are distributed as follows: 14 Church Slavonic texts, 4 texts in Church Slavonic with added parts in Ukrainian, one bilingual edition, the rest in "simple" (usually Ukrainian) language[50].

8. When Fedorov died in L'viv in 1583, the *Uspens'ke bratstvo* (Assumption Brotherhood), took over Fedorov's press and founded his own printing house. At that time, the Ukrainian Fraternities played a vital role, defending of the cities burghers' rights and the Orthodox faith. The press, schooling and charity were three closely related spheres of the Brotherhood's activities in L'viv. In 1592 the Brotherhood obtained the monopoly of printing Cyrillic church and school books from the Polish king; the director of the press house was the monk Minna, Fedorov's close collaborator helped by Fedorov's son and by Hryn' Ivanovyč. In the XVI century, the main publication of the house was a Greek and Church Slavonic grammar, *Adelphotes* (1591)[51], used in the Brotherhood school (182 leaves).

The Church hierarchy attempted to subdue the Brotherhood publishing and put it under its control: on 26 October, 1591, the orthodox bishops decided at the Cathedral of Brest that Vilnius and L'viv Brotherhoods were to print only the texts authorized by the bishops. To avoid the control of local bishops, L'viv Brotherhood strengthened direct contacts with the Metropolitan of Kyïv and the Eastern Patriarchs. And in 1593 it assumed the name of "Stavropigian", granted

---

49 A copy is available in NLVUK.
50 Isajevyč 2002, p. 138.
51 A copy is available in MLS.

by the Patriarch of Constantinople.[52] However, by that time the L'viv Brotherhood's printing activity had apparently come to a halt. No publication from 1594-1608 has been preserved that could be definitely attributed to this printer. The prohibition for Orthodox congregations to publish books without bishops' authorization lost validity as almost all the bishops accepted the Union of Brest. Among the sixteen known Fraternity publications issued over the first 25 years (1591-1616) of its activity, there were only four liturgical books, a sign of the publishers' prevalent social and lay interests.

Since the printing press did not bring significant profits, it was not restored after a fire that damaged the building. Due to the general decline in activity, Brotherhood's most famous printing and school staff went to work in Kyïv; here, about 1615 there were the Lavra Monastery printing and a local Brotherhood with own school. In 1617-1629 L'viv Brotherhood printing was not active[53], but afterwards it recovered and remained in existence until 1939.

9. According to an ancient opinion, which dates back at least to the XVIII century, the characters and instrumentation for printing passed from Ostroh to Kyïv Pečers'ka Lavra; but the Kyïvian font, although similar the Ostrohian, is not identical with it. The most ancient Kyïvian edition are *The Book of Hours* (about 1616)[54] and a poetic panegyric in Ukrainian of Lavra's Archimandrite, Jelysej Pletenec'kyj (who led the Monastery from 1599 until his death in 1624), written by Oleksandr Mytura (1618)[55]. Following an incorrect (as Maslov stressed)[56] list of the nineteenth century, Titov wrongly assumed in his book on the Lavra's typography that the press enterprise had started in 1606. But the very preface of the *The Book of Hours* names it the first-born of Kyïv publishing, while the Pletenec'kyj panegyric says that the Archimandrite bought the fonts and the printing equipments owned by the ancient bishop of L'viv, Hedeon Bala-

---

52 In Orthodox Christianity, "Stavropigian" designates an institution or a monastery that is answerable to a Metropolitan's or a Patriarch's direct jurisdiction, rather than to that of a diocesan bishop.
53 Isajevyč 2002, p. 146.
54 A copy is available in MLS.
55 A copy is available in MLS.
56 Maslov 1924, p. 45.

ban, who died in 1607[57]. Balaban, in fact, had tried to compete with the Brotherhood printing by setting up his own office in the town of Stryatyn[58].

The first major Lavra-edited volume was an *Anfolohion* [*Menaion*][59], released in January 1619. It counted 16 unnumbered and 1648 numbered pages *in folio*. The text was deliberately commissioned in small print (10 lines - 49 mm). It is interesting to note that some press notes placed on the sheets allow us to calculate the time required for printing: 12 - 14.5 pages per week. The selection of the Propers shows the publishers' intentions to use the cult of local saints to emphasize the role of Kyïv in the life of the nation and within the Orthodox world: the book includes liturgies of the nobles Kyïvian Saints (the *knjazi* Volodymyr, Borys and Hlib), of the Blessed Antonij and Feodosij of the Caves, of the Metropolitans Petro and Oleksij, of the Apostol Andrew (who was said to have predicted the future role of Kyïv), of the popular Saints Paraskevi of Iconium and Onufrij, of the prophet Elisha and of the Great Martyr Euphemia - patrons of Pletenec'kyj[60]. Among the editions of the early period of Cave printing there is *Virši...* (*A Poem*)[61] in memory of Petro Konaševyč-Sahajdačnyj, Het'man of the Cossacks; it was composed (1622) by Kasijan Sakovyč, a monk and the rector of the Kyïvian Brotherhood schools. Sahajdačnyj had played an important role in the restoration of the Metropolitan See of Kyïv and in the emergence of Cossacks as a unified political power. According to Isajevyč,

the book is very interesting because it contains historical and ordinary details; in it patriotic motives resonated in a full voice. For the first time in the practice of Cyrillic typography there are secular illustrations: an equestrian portrait of Sahajdačnyj, an attack of the Cossack fleet on the Turkish fortress of Kaffa, in Crimea[62].

Of course, the Lavra's liturgical texts and prayer books were almost all printed in Church Slavonic. A very significant exception is, in part, *Triod' pisna* [*Lenten Triodion*] of 1627[63], which Tarasij Zem-

---

57 Ohijenko 1994, pp. 257-259.
58 *Ibid.*, pp. 164-170.
59 Copies are available in NLVUK and MSL.
60 Isajevyč 2002, p. 170.
61 A Copy is available in MLS.
62 Isajevyč 2002, p. 172.
63 Copies are available in NLVUK and MSL.

ka translated into Ukrainian. This *Triod'* was the most richly illustrated Ukrainian book of the first half of the XVII century (125 illustrations with 84 boards). In autumn 1627, the printing was completed of Pamva Berynda's famous *Leksykon Slavenoros'kyj*[64], which exerted a sustained influence on the development of the East Slavic lexicography. The dictionary consists of two parts: the first contains translation of words from Church Slavonic into Ukrainian, and the second comprises explanations of Biblical personal and place names.

With the election, in the same year, of Petro Mohyla as Lavra Archimandrite, who afterward became also Metropolitan of Kyïv and founded the glorious Kyïvian Academy, the Lavra became the main Ukrainian and Eastern Orthodox publisher (1650-1720). Around 1650, for example, Tsar Alexis I promoted the publication in the Muscovite realm of the Kyïvian theological works, including the Profession of Faith written by Mohyla; a trend that grew with the election in 1652 of the Patriarch Nikon, a reformist.

But in 1720's, the situation changed radically. After Mazepa attempted a secession, Russian government banned publications of Kyïvian and Černihiv printers other than reprints of old books, which had to be in Russian and even with the same Russian accents. Around the time when Kyïv and Černihiv printing came under devastating and humiliating control of the Russian government and of the Russian Church, the L'viv Brotherhood's printing was placed under the control of the papal Nuncio and his designated commissioners[65]. However, their supervision were not as pervasive as the draconian Russian measures for the Hetmanate, where the Kyïv and Černihiv printing office (the latter generally stopped working and was restored in 1743) confined their ventures to the art of book design and reprinting of prayer books. The Mohylian Academy had to resort to having some of its materials printed abroad, especially in Germany[66]. In 1767 the governor of the imperial Slobožanščyna asked the Russian Senate for the permission to establish a printing press at the College of Charkiv, but his request was rejected[67].

---

64 Copies are available in NLVUK and MSL.
65 Ohijenko 1994, p. 298; Isajevyč 2002, p. 232.
66 Isajevyč 2002, p. 262.
67 *Ibid.*, p. 293.

10. In the foregoing, we have extensively summarized the Ukrainian historiography of Ukrainian early print culture. In interpretative perspective, we have seen at least 5 narrative assumptions at work in the Ukrainian historiography of this phenomenon: 1. The rebuttal of the pan-Russian rhetoric, accepted by both Russian nationalists and Soviets, in which Ukraine and Belarus are framed as two components of the greater Russian nation; consequently, the history of printing in Ukraine cannot fall within a broader history of Russian printing or Cyrillic printing. Indeed, it is the Ukrainian land that has given birth to printing in Cyrillic characters. 2. The existence, from the XI century on, of a Ukrainian ethnic-territorial space and of a Ukrainian cultural world. 3. The emphasis on a Ukrainian tinge in the Church Slavonic of the first books printed in Cyrillic. 4. The emphasis, on the other hand, on the shared life of Ukrainians and Belarusians in the times of the Grand Duchy of Lithuania. 5. The refusal of a rhetorical Polish narration, which, as Isajevyč claims, "subsumes all Ukrainian and Belarusian who worked in the *Rzeczpospolita* among 'Polish books editors', even those who were given the Orthodox Church Slavonic liturgical books"[68].

All of these assumptions (some to a lesser and some to a greater extent, as we have seen) are shareable and justified but must be viewed in the context of international factors which contributed to the birth and development of Ukrainian printing. Sometimes, when this international conjuncture is not adequately emphasized, Ukrainian historiography tends to Ukrainise all of early printing in Cyrillic. We certainly can affirm that Ukrainian space must be considered the cradle of printing in Cyrillic characters, but the Polish and the Belarusian impact must not be overlooked. In addition, the presence of German and Russian craftsmen in the printing enterprises makes it necessary to accept the multinational and complex character of Ukrainian printing at the onset of the Early Modern period. Soon afterwards, the high-quality printing activities of the Brotherhood of L'viv and of the Kyïv Pečers'ka Lavra prevailed as sources of dissemination of Orthodox-Ruthenian-Ukrainian print culture, in interaction with Polish and Latin culture of the *Rzeczpospolita* as well in conjunction with other Orthodox Slavic countries where printing was less developed, such as Muscovite Russia.

---

68 *Ibid.*, p. 36.

BIBLIOGRAPHY

S. Baillie, *Introduction* to Wynar 1962.

D. Brandenberger, *National Bolshevism*. Cambridge, Mass. 2002.

I.D. Hoffmann, *De typographiis earumque initiis et incrementis in Regno Poloniae et Magno Ducatu Lithuaniae*, Gdańsk 1740.

M. Hrushevsky, *The Traditional Scheme of "Russian" History and the Problem of a Rational Organization of the History of the East Slavs*, in L. R. Wynar, *Mykhailo Hrushevsky: Ukrainian-Russian Confrontation in Historiography*, Toronto-New York-Munich 1988, pp. 35-42.

I. Karataev, *Opisanie slavjano-russkich knig napečatannyx kirillovskimi bukvami* [*Description of the Slavic-Russian Books Printed with Cyrillc Characters*], Vol. I, *1491-1752*, St. Petersburg 1883.

J. Isajevyč, *Ukraïns'ke Knyhovydannja: vytoky, rozvytok, problemy* [*The Ukrainian Publishing; Origins, Development, Problems*], L'viv 2002.

R. Jakobson, "Ivan Fedorov's *Primer*", *Harvard Library Bullettin*, 9, 1955, pp. 5-39.

K. Lambrecht, "Aufstiegschancen und Handlungsräume in Ostmitteleuropäischen Zentren um 1500: Das Beispiel Der Unternehmerfamilie Thurzo", *Zeitschrift für Ostmitteleuropa-Forschung*, 47, 1998, pp. 317-346.

M. Maksimovič, *Knižnaja starina južnorusskaja* [*Antique Books of the Southern Russia*], in *Sobranie sočinenij* [*Collected Works*], t. 3, Kyïv 1880.

S. Maslov, *Drukarstvo na Ukraïni v XVI—XVIII st.* [*Printing in Ukraine in the XVI-XVII century*], Kyïv 1924.

I. Ohijenko, *Istorija Ukraïns'koho Drukarstva* [*A History of Ukrainian Printing*], Kyïv 1994 (second edition).

J. Ptasnik (ed.), *Cracovia impressorum XV et XVI ss.*, L'viv 1922.

F.I. Titov, *Tipografija Kievo-Pečerskoj Lavry. Istoričeskij očerk* [*The Typography of Kyïv Pečers'ka Lavra. Historical Essay*], Kyïv 1918.

S. Tomanovič, "Die erste slavisch-cyrillische Buchdruckerei", *Centralblatt für Bibliothekswesen*, XVII, 1900, pp. 429-431.

L.R. Wynar, *History of Early Ukrainian Printing. 1491-1600*, Denver 1962.

D. Zubrzycki, *Historyczne badania o drukarniach rusko-słowiańskich w Galicyi* [*Historical research about Russian-Slavic printing in Galicia*], L'viv 1836.

3. The Prologue *to the* Narcissus *of Hryhorij Skovoroda: A Synthesis of the Modern Ukrainian Culture*

This essay is a version of my paper read at the Colloquium "Poetics of Selfhood: writing and other constructions", Faculdade de Letras of the University of Lisbon, 3-5 March 2014; an amended version should be published in the next issue - 2, 2015 - of "Kyiv-Mohyla Humanities Journal".

1. The composition of the dialogue *Narcissus. A Deliberation on the Topic: Know Thyself* followed a complex itinerary; the dialogue, written in the years 1769-1771 (i.e. two years after the abandonment of the teaching post at the College of Charkiv),constitutes one of the first of Skovoroda's philosophical works[1]; previously, after about 1750, he had written poems, apologues, moral fables and a didactic treatise. At the end of his life, in 1794, Skovoroda wished to precede with a *Prologue (Prolog)*[2] his beloved philosophical "first child" (as he calls it)[3], which assumes the meaning of a true philosophical testament.

We have two autograph copies of the dialogue; the Prologue is not present in them and the name of Narcissus appears neither in the title nor in the text. The inclusion of the name of Narcissus (Narkiss)

---

1 In 1768, Skovoroda had drafted a treaty of ethics (*The Primary Door to Christian Ethics*) which he used as a textbook for the course which he held at the theological College of Charkiv; disagreements with the episcopal authority on the content of the treaty led Skovoroda to leave his post and to abandon teaching. Unclear is the timing of another dialogue entitled *A Symphony Called the Book of Askhan of Self-Knowledge*; according to Uškalov (cf. Skovoroda 2011, p. 346) and other scholars it was written shortly after the composition of the *Narcissus*.

2 "Feci Prologon et in «Narcissum», id est, in Librum: «NOSCE TE IPSUM»." Letter to M. Kovalyns'kyj, 2 april 1794, in Skovoroda 2011, p. 1186.

3 This is said at the beginning of the Prologue, repeating what Skovoroda had already written in a letter of 1790 (cf. Letter to M. Kovalyns'kyj of 26 September 1790, in Skovoroda 2011, p. 1185).

in the title came from a letter of 1790 to Mychajlo Kovalyns'kyj in which Skovoroda claims to have found the text of the dialogue among the papers of a friend of his, a priest[4]; thus the new entitling should date back to a time just after the preparation of the second autograph copy, which was not composed before the end of 1788[5], while the Prologue should not be, as mentioned, prior to 1793-4.

It is to be noted that the works of Skovoroda are calligraphic manuscripts; their publication in print was posthumous. From 1720, the Russian authorities (after the attempted secession of Mazepa) applied strict control over the printing in the part of Ukraine under the Hetmanate, allowing only reprints. In 1767 the governor of Slobožanščyna had asked the Senate imperial permission to set up a printing press at the College of Charkiv, receiving a rejection[6]. In such conditions, to which is added the isolation of Skovoroda from educational or religious institutions, writing for publication was not even contemplated.

It was therefore not until 1798 that the first edition (incomplete) of *Narcissus*, which also represented the first of Skovoroda's work to be printed, was published in St. Petersburg; the dialogue was published anonymously and with a different title, by the imperial librarian and historian Mychajlo Antonovs'kyj, a Freemason and a former student of the Mohylian Academy. Important components of the first Russian Masonic movement were animated by a strong spirituality of Christian origin[7] which had significant elements of affinity with the inner asceticism proposed by Skovoroda, made known to the Petersburger Freemasons by Ukrainian affiliates[8]; close to Freemasonry we also find Kovalyns'kyj.[9] We may exclude, however, any form of affiliation on Skovoroda's part to Freemasonry, both for his natural shyness for any organization, and for his repeated hostility to "sects"; authoritative scholars as Jefremov and Sumcov also excluded his membership,

---

4 Cf. Letter to M. Kovalyns'kyj of 26 September 1790, p. 1186.
5 On autographed copies and their dating it is useful to consult the critical edition of the Skovoroda's works of 1973: Skovoroda 1973, pp. 498-499. There are also six manuscript copies of the autographs (one of which is preserved in Romania).
6 Isajevyč 2002, p. 293.
7 On the late eighteenth century Russian Freemasonry see: Faggionato 2005.
8 Uškalov 2006, p. 150.
9 The same applies to the other favorite pupil of Skovoroda's, Vasyl' Tomara; see: Uškalov 2004, p. 99. Tomara, who was the first private student of Skovoroda, who lived in the house of his father for a few years, pursued an important career in imperial administration and then appeared as one of the participants in the conversation described in De Maistre's *St. Petersburg Dialogues*.

although both see contact points between the doctrines of Skovoroda and those of Russians Freemasons[10]. On the other hand, Kovalyns'kyj reports that Skovoroda said: "I do not know the Martinists, their reasoning or their teachings"[11].

2. The figure of Narcissus is unusually positive, for Skovoroda, and connected to the theme of "know thyself" declined in the Augustinian sense. He was driven, conceiving this association, by an iconographic tradition, which can be traced back to certain late medieval representations of Narcissus as a symbol of the contemplative life[12]; this image then flowed into certain texts of emblems of the modern era and was associated in two known cases to the Delphic-Socratic motto. We know the importance of the emblematic in Renaissance and Baroque[13]; even in the Kyïvian Academy the emblematic was held in high regard. The typography of the institute had printed several volumes of emblems, while in private libraries of the leading Ukrainian intellectuals there were several emblematic encyclopedias published in the West, as in that of Stefan Javor'skyj (which then went on to form the main part of the library of the College of Charkiv)[14]. Skovoroda participated in this taste of his era and liked to illustrate his autograph with symbols and emblems, whose power of condensation and conceptual expression he greatly esteemed. He writes in the Introduction to the *Fables of Charkov* (1774):

no color can describe the rose, the lily, narcissus in such a vivid way as the aura of celestial and terrestrial images which the invisible divine truth wonderfully creates in them, whence were born *hieroglyphica*, *emblemata*, *symbola*, mysteries, parables, fables, similes, proverbs[15].

In 1788 in St. Petersburg the new edition of the only Russian text of emblems was issued, and Skovoroda was definitely able to consult it while attending the patrician houses of Slobožanščyna; among the nobles who gave him hospitality there was, for example, the deputy

---

10 Cf. Sumcov 1886; Jefremov 2009, p. 169.
11 Kovalyns'kyj 2011, p. 1368. Russians Freemasons were sometimes called "Martinists" for their appreciation for the French theosophist Louis Claude de Saint-Martin.
12 Uguccioni 1993.
13 Cf. Praz 1974.
14 Uškalov 2011, p. 36.
15 Skovoroda 2011, p. 155. On symbolism in Skovoroda see: Čyževs'kyj 1934, pp. 26-49.

governor of the province, in whose house Skovoroda actually lived in the last months of his life. The 1788 edition of the book, issued with the title (changed from the previous edition) *Emvlemy i simvoly*, was addressed directly to the spread of noble and public heraldry among the aristocrats and among state officials.[16] However, Skovoroda surely already knew the first edition of the book, printed in Amsterdam in 1705 by order of Peter the Great, as he copied by hand and inserted in the dialogue *Alfavit* (1775)[17] emblem n. 718[18], which is entitled "Narcissus" and subtitled "Know thyself."

The first edition of the book was addressed specifically to artists and naval craftsmen. It was a sort of emblematic encyclopedia commissioned by the Tsar to a Dutch printer and edited by the Russian-speaking Pole, Elias Kopijewski[19]; almost exclusive sources of the book were two works published just before in Amsterdam by Daniel de la Feuille, who in turn used emblems found in previous collections. In particular, the emblems numbered 709 to 840 of the Russian collection reproduced those of *Devises et emblemes d'amour*, published in 1696 by de la Feuille under the pseudonym Giuseppe Pallavicini[20]; among the sources used for the latter work, the one linking the figure of Narcissus to the Delphic motto is *Thronus Cupidinis* published in Amsterdam in 1618 and reissued in 1620. In *Thronus* symbol n. 29 is entitled "Nosce te ipsum" and depicts Narcissus, who is mirroring himself in a stream; a commentary in Latin refers to the usual overestimation of the self that afflicts humans. In previous emblematic literature, another known case in which there was an association between the Delphic motto and the figure of Narcissus is *Emblemata. Partim Ethica Et Physica, Partim vero Historica & Hieroglyphica* of Nikolaus Resner, published in Frankfurt in 1581[21]; the image is in Book III of the text, in the emblem XXVI on page 137, and wishes to warn against pride.

The date of publication of the *Emvlemy i simvoly* (1788) and the decision to give a new title to his first dialogue (1790), lead us to as-

---

16 Hippisley 1989, pp. XXXIII and passim.
17 Skovoroda 2011, p. 686.
18 *Symbola et emblemata* 1705, pp. 240-241.
19 A reprint of the book had been made in 1743, as many copies had been lost; see: Čyževs'kyj 1994, p. 44.
20 On the iconographic sources of *Emblemy i simvoly* see: Hippisley 1989, pp. XIV and passim.
21 Ordine 2003, pp. 194-195.

sume that the renewed vision of the emblem of the Russian collection suggested to Skovoroda the new title and the figure of the protagonist of the Prologue. It was not, on the other hand, an extrinsic solution because the dialogue, while never referring to Narcissus, encouraged self-knowledge. On the other hand, Skovoroda changed the symbolic relationship suggested by the emblematic iconography we have mentioned: his Narcissus was no longer merely the symbol of self-love or of the encouragement to know oneself in order to tame the instincts of pride, but it became the protagonist of the main message of his philosophy, namely the passionate *indiamento* (deification). It is a mature fruit of his reflection; as in *Alfavit,* the portrayal of Narcissus was traditional, that is, one who is deceived by exterior images and does not understand the need to know oneself[22]. The originality of Skovoroda's new choice is accentuated by the absence of reference to Narcisuss in Neoplatonic literature and Christian Neoplatonism, unless in a negative sense and never in association with the theme of self-knowledge. In the literature of the Ruthenian Baroque, little accustomed to erotic themes[23], there is only one previous use of the figure of Narcissus[24], which helps to make Skovoroda's Narcissus even more original.

3. In the Prologue to the *Narkiss*, Skovoroda then does not follow, except marginally, the plot of deception and death that afflicts the protagonist of Ovid's poem. He also does not appear affected by the negative symbolism that, in Plotinus and Ficino, makes Narcissus the victim of his fatal mistake in thinking that the uncertain and material world is the real world. The death of Narcissus, in Skovoroda, is a joyful metamorphosis, as he says in the *Prologue*: "Oh my dear beloved Narcissus! Now from a creeping caterpillar you have arisen as a winged butterfly. You have been resurrected!"[25]. It is therefore a step on the road to *indiamento*, while self-love is not stigmatized; on the contrary, it is considered a necessary moment in the journey towards truth, through a miracle:

---

22 Skovoroda 2011, pp. 686-687.
23 Pylypiuk 1997, p. 35.
24 By Stefan Javors'kyj (Jaworski), cited by Uškalov in H. Skovoroda 2011, p. 272.
25 Skovoroda 2011, p. 232.

The miracle that appeared in the waters to Narcissus.
Tell me, O beautiful Narcissus,did you see something in your waters? Did someone appear?
RESPONSE. In my waters (…) I beheld on the linen cloth of my body which
flowed, an image not created by human hand (…). My flesh is the enchantress who
showed me my Samuel. I love this one, and I melt, I disappear, I am transformed[26].

This setting, as well as being very original for the symbolism of Narcissus, puts the relationship between man and God, between creature and principle, in terms which are quite different from those of Ficino and Plotinus, who are the most important theoretical references of the theme of *indiamento* (although Skovoroda's interest in their work does not seem to be significant). In Plotinus there prevails a certain "automatism", of an emanationistic nature, in the return of the creature to the Principle, given the neither creationist nor personal nature of the individual soul in the Neoplatonic processional scheme; it follows, among other things, that the soul yearns, in Plotinus' view, not so much for unification, as a reunification with the principle that cancels itself[27]. In Ficino, on the other hand, there is a kind of "spontaneous" ascent on the part of the soul, which, having abandoned the outside world and recognized itself as spirit, by the virtue of divine grace rises to ideas and then to God[28].

In Skovoroda there is the theme, absent in his predecessors, of self-love, which is a strong ethical and personal commitment; then, in Skovoroda, awareness of the ideal nature of the real seems to precede and produce the recognition of the spiritual nature of man. This primacy of knowledge (and ethics) over deductive ontology, which is significantly supported by the fact that in his writings Skovoroda mentions at least thirty times Plato (sometimes quoting directly from his works) and never Plotinus, as well as having a premise in Augustine, can be explained by a kind of philosophical modernism on the part of the Ukrainian thinker, who was no stranger to the themes of the Enlightenment[29] and certainly has introjected the epistemologism of modern (Cartesian-Leibnizian) philosophy[30].

---

26 *Ibid.*, p. 233.
27 Arnou 1921.
28 This difference does not seems to emerge in Pič 1995, which presents Skovoroda's *indiamento* as almost identical to that of Plotinus; see, especially, pages 164-167.
29 Scherer 2008.
30 On the modern rationalism in the Kyïvian Academy in the eighteenth century, see: Ničyk

Platonism is clearly stated in *Prolog*, citing the "Book of Daniel": "So you do not know that the outward appearance, the face, the flesh, the idol amounted to nothing? Do you not know, then, that this world is the idol of the Dura Plain?"[31]. The dialogue, especially in its first part, was animated by Platonic demonstration of the transience of opinions and feelings and the sense of truth inherent in rising to the ideal world. It began, in the first conversation featuring the skeptic Luke and the Friend (aka Skovoroda), by denying validity to sensitive knowledge:

You, of course, know without a doubt that our eyes, ears, tongues, hands, feet and entire body accomplish nothing by themselves, but are completely enslaved by our thoughts. Thought (...) reasons, advises, makes definitions, commands. But our limited flesh, like a harnessed beast or tail, follows it willy-nilly. So you see that thought is our principal and central element[32].

Platonian is also the theme of the difficulty of getting out of the "cave" of opinions and sensitive certainties: "counsel only develops slowly. Ah! the earth is sticky. One cannot quickly remove his foot from the sticky, carnal way of thinking. Having developed early in us, it is rightly called superstition."[33] Luke (the skeptic) admits in the fifth conversation: "an ingrained opinion is like the infant who grew into a giant"[34].

In the second conversation, to help the desire expressed by Luka to leave the darkness of sensitivity, the Friend advances some Pythagorean-Platonic conceptual demonstrations, also the result of an implicit awareness of the mathematical Platonism that supports the metaphysics of modern science. Before a mural painting, the friend asks Luke:

Friend. Tell me, what do you consider to be painting? The colors or the drawing hidden in the colors?
Luke. The colors are not anything but dust and emptiness; the drawing, or the proportion and arrangement of the colors, that is the strength. But if that is missing, then the colors are simply filth and emptiness[35].

2001.
31 Skovoroda 2011, p. 232.
32 *Ibid.*, p. 236.
33 *Ibid.*, p. 237.
34 *Ibid.*, p. 252.
35 *Ibid.*, p. 239.

Widening the example to the building of a church, the Friend goes on to note that there is a general relationship between the symmetries, i.e. a project that is not only geometrical, but also takes on ethical and religious significance:

Friend. if you see an old church in Achtyrka of brick and lime, but do not understand its plan, how do you think you have perceived and known it?
Luke. Not at all! In this fashion I see only the extreme and worst externality in it, which a beast sees, but its symmetry or proportion and plan, which is the connection and principle to all the material, insofar as I do not understand that, I do not see it, because I have not seen its principle. (…)
Friend. So why do you not perceive that the unseen takes precedence in other creatures and not only in man? (…) Spirit sculpts everything-in-everything[36].

Having established the principles of a Platonic epistemology, there follows a cornerstone of Skovoroda's metaphysics, namely the dual nature of the world, which has tones of a Stoic revised version of Plato's *Timaeus*: "The whole world consists of two NATURES: one visible, the other invisible. The visible is called creation, but the invisible is called God. This invisible nature, or God, permeates and sustains all creation; it was, is and will be, always and everywhere"[37].

4. The discovery of spirituality is also for Skovoroda a personal *event*, to experience through knowledge and acceptance of one's inner self. Here we have a clear roadmap for Narcissus, as Skovoroda summarizes in *Prolog*: "Whoever has seen clearly in the water the beauty of his own decay, has become enamored not by externality or putrefaction, but by himself, by his own most essential point [*točka*]"[38]. At the beginning of the fourth conversation in the dialogue, the Friend had already warned of the importance of this exceptional work on themselves, saying, inspired by St. Paul: "true man and God are the same"[39]. Self-love, then, is the premise for the union with the Source of being, as the *Prologue* announces:

My Narcissus, indeed, burns, being kindled with the fire of love (…). He cares for and talks about not multifarious or empty things, but about, for and in himself. He

---

36 *Ibid.*, p. 240.
37 *Ibid.*, p. 253.
38 *Ibid.*, p. 231.
39 *Ibid.*, p. 246.

42

cares only about himself. That single thing is all he needs. Finally, all of him, like ice melting in the fire of self-love, is transformed into the source. Truly! Truly! Of whatever one has become enamored, into that he will be transformed. Everyone is that whose heart is in him. Everyone is where his heart is[40].

So, having discovered himself as a person and drawn from the ideal nature of truth, man is ready to meet God, which is realized in the meditation of the "third world", that is, the Bible, as Skovoroda explains in his last dialogue (*The Serpent's Flood*, 1790):

There are three worlds. The first is the common and inhabited world, where lives every being that is born. It consists of innumerable worlds of worlds, and is the larger world. The other two are the small and partial worlds. The one is the microcosm, that is, the small world or man. The other is the symbolic world, namely the Bible[41].

This is not a path that has a real term, since the activity of interpretation of the symbols is inexhaustible: God, according to a famous metaphor of Skovoroda (contained in *Silenus Alcibiadis*, 1775), is as an elusive bird a hermit was in love with; "the bird, approaching on purpose, urged him to chase it and a thousand times it seemed to rest in his hands, but he could never catch it"[42].

Narcissus, in the *Prologue*, confirms the possibility of this conceptual and personal route, emphasizing its mystic outcomes:

Narcissus: I love the source and the mouth, the spring and the BEGINNING, the eternal streams which issue from the vapor of its own heart. The sea is decay. Rivers pass. Currents dry up. Streams disappear. The source breathes eternally with the vapor which vitalizes and refreshes. I love the source ALONE and disappear into it. For me everything else is the sewer, trash, dirt, a shadow and the tail...[43]

5. Skovoroda's original theme of the self as a means for *indiamento* made him close to Bruno's "frenzied one" for his vicissitudes, as a means to elevate to a "burning contact" with God. Giordano Bruno seems to be one of the modern authors more akin to Skovoroda, for themes touched on, ontological solutions and lifestyle, although there are also very marked differences between the two. This theme

---

40 *Ibid.*, p. 231.
41 H. Skovoroda, *Dialog. Imja emu: Potop zmiin*, in Skovoroda 2011, p. 968.
42 H. Skovoroda, *Knižečka, nazyvaemaja Silenus Alcibiadis*, in Skovoroda 2011, p. 735.
43 Skovoroda 2011, p. 232.

of influences and affinities in Bruno's thought on Skovoroda has only been mentioned by a few scholars[44], but never probed or dealt with in depth.

It is hard to say how familiar Skovoroda was with the philosophy of Bruno: probably not beyond a general knowledge related to the reputation of Bruno revived by Toland at the beginning of the eighteenth century and which penetrated in the German circles of Wolff and his school[45], from which Konys'kyj probably took his knowledge that he divulged in the Mohylian Academy[46]; texts of Bruno would be owned by the library of the Academy.[47] Finally, Skovoroda often cites "the Copernican worlds", perhaps because he had read the Russian translation of Huygens' *Cosmotheoros* (which appeared in 1714)[48], in which Bruno is mentioned alongside Cusano as a theoretic of the universe's infinity. We, however, have no record of the fact that the Ukrainian philosopher meditated on Bruno's doctrines. We must assume, therefore, a spontaneous convergence of Skovoroda and Bruno on similar themes, based on independent speculative itineraries, as indeed often happened in that age-old Neoplatonic tradition in which the two thinkers worked.

Bruno's mixture of naturalism and Hermeticism, which ontologically supports the protagonism of Bruno's "frenzied one", is foreign to Skovoroda, for whom the *prisca theologia* is valued not in view of Bruno's "Egyptian", solar and anti-Christian reform[49], but in that of the Christian *philosophia perennis*, of Steuco, Ficino and Leibniz[50]. Not surprisingly, in the first lines of the *Prolog* Skovoroda attributes the origin of the "parable" of Narcissus not to Ovid, but to "Egyptian theology", which, he immediately adds, "is the mother of the Jewish one"[51] stating that there is a sequence relationship not an opposition.

Moreover, we do not find in Skovoroda the whole tragic plot that characterizes the efforts of Bruno's "frenzied one", who is moved to the truth by the "vicious" refusal of peace and temperance, which in

---

44 Frank 1910.

45 Ricci 1990, pp. 242-244; 366-367.

46 Kašuba 1972.

47 They were part, along with those of many other Modern authors, of a legacy of Prokopovyč; see: Niženec' 1970, p. 25.

48 Scherer 1997, p. 56.

49 Yates 1964.

50 On Skovoroda and the *philosophia perennis* see: von Erdmann 2005.

51 Skovoroda 2011, p. 231.

turn leads him to want the truth so much as to *hate himself*[52]. Not surprisingly, Bruno's "frenzied one" is best represented by Actaeon, who ended up devoured, because the fate of Bruno's "frenzied one" is unfortunate in the sense that he must burn in the fire of love, die or become blind, and long suffer this condition, before having the final illumination and ecstatic contact with the truth.

At the center of all Skovoroda's philosophical efforts there is, instead, a tapping, not so much of suffering and transfiguring illumination, but of happiness and balance and therefore an enhancement of Hellenistic ethics, the *tranquillitas* which is associated with the *art of life* and the pursuit of happiness. He is in fact known to have professed an original[53] Christian Epicureanism which brought him to support a bold parallelism between Epicurus and Christ. The origins of this approach are in the suggestions from *Colloquia familiaria* of Erasmus (a book owned by the College of Charkiv and definitely cherished by Skovoroda)[54], and in some ideas present in Basil of Caesarea and Clement of Alexandria, in addition to the affection Konys'kyj felt for Epicurus[55]. Against Bruno's dramaticism, plays another Epicurean element, namely the accessibility and naturalness of good, which in the *Prolog* is confirmed by the following passage: "thanks be to the blessed God. It is His ineffable grace and power which makes the useless impossible and the possible useful"[56].

Skovoroda however does not seek a mere detached happiness, without discomposure, but a joyful *tranquillitas*, that goes beyond mere Epicureanism, in the direction of a Middle Platonian and Christian correction - in the wake of Plutarch, Philo and Basil - of the Epicurean ataraxia. In fact, the theme of the "joy of the heart" (*radost' serdca*) as the purpose of life, and not a mere equanimity, often returns in the works of Skovoroda who, in a letter of 1765 to Kovalyns'kyj, writes clearly: "nihil curare, nihil dolere non est vivere sed mortuum esse: cura enim est animi motu et vita in motu consistit"[57]. Even early Stoicism's *apatheia* is explicitly rejected by Skovoroda, who believes

---

52 Bruno 2000, p. 799.
53 Ruthenian theology was generally anti-Epicurean; see Uškalov 1999, pp. 129-130.
54 See the note of Uškalov in Skovoroda 2011, p. 115. On the influence of Erasmus on Skovoroda, see: Pylypiuk 1990.
55 Cf. Bartolini 2007.
56 Skovoroda 2011, p. 233.
57 Letter to M. Kovalyns'kyj, August 1765, in Skovoroda 2011, p. 1177.

that passions can cooperate in achieving happiness: "Ergo, inquis, cum Stoicis postulas tu sapientem prorsus ἀπαθέα esse? Imo vero sic stipes erit, non homo. Restat igitur, ut ibi sit beatitudo, ubi moderatio, non ubi affectuum vacation."[58] The state of active joy consists in indulging *srodnost'*, that is, authenticity or affinity. This part of Skovoroda's anthropology was developed in the aforementioned dialogue *Alfavit*, which proclaims the fundamental principle: "without affinity, everything is nothing." It is a perspective that values all individuality, which is treated as an individual substance in the plot of being, almost Scotus's *haecceitas*: "There are a hundred affinities, and a hundred conditions, all reputable and legitimate"[59]. The right job, the right occupation is the culmination of the joy and of active human presence in the world[60]. Knowledge and action are therefore the means by which we reach happiness, which is nothing but the full realization of our potential[61].

In essence, while using a eudemonistic language, Skovoroda's moral philosophy cannot be called a form of Christian eudemonism. There are those who, rightly, have compared it to today's personalism, so Skovoroda's indiamento must also be seen as a call to pursue a self-construction that goes along with personal authenticity and that one profuses into a positive social activity.

6. It must be said, therefore, that the sources of Skovoroda's *indiamento* are not Bruno's, but go back to the Neoplatonic Patristic, corrected by Stoic themes; in addition, there are obvious influences from the Slavic-Byzantine religious tradition, but they are not dominant, because the Kyïvian College had marked a conversion of Ukrainian cultural life by a prevailing Slavic-Byzantine matrix to the Slavic-Latin. The Byzantine influence continued to be used throughout the liturgy against a background of mystical sensibility. On the other hand, compared to the so-called Western Second Scholastic, under whose influence it came, the Mohylian College had both greater openness with respect to Renaissance Humanism, the Reformation or Enlightenment themes, and greater flexibility than the Western theological strands.

---

58 Letter to M. Kovalyns'kyj, winter 1763, in Skovoroda 2011, p. 1118.
59 Skovoroda 2011, p. 654.
60 *Ibid.*, p. 651.
61 Zakydalsky 1994, pp. 242-243.

Self-knowledge is part of the "natural" cycle of things and being, as in the Stoic language, that binds the universal generator Fire and the individual fire or hegemonic. Skovoroda clarifies the fact in the *Dialogue Among Five Travelers* (1772) that the best way to call God is to call him "nature." "*Natura* is the Latin word which is equivalent to our terms nature and substance"[62]. In the sense, as he had stated in *Narkiss*, that "He Himself is the principle, and is all in all"[63].

There are few and fragmentary works on the relationship between Skovoroda and Stoicism; it is the exegete who has to rebuild it, since there are no decisive signs in Skovoroda on this point, important though it is. On the other hand, it was especially Neoplatonism (and not so much Stoicism) which accentuated the theme of "return" to God and the chance to do this by retreating into oneself: in *Enneads* Plotinus had said: "with our center we come into contact with the center of everything" (VI 9, 8). Endre von Ivánka has shown how Neoplatonism absorbed and spiritualized the Stoic ontological scheme of an originating Fire from which the other bodies descend, for cooling and removal; an outcome that had its premises in Cicero and then in the attempt made by Middle Platonism, in the first centuries of the Christian era, to give a Platonic content to the dominant Stoic philosophy[64]. Skovoroda had definitely drawn from his beloved Plutarch an attitude of this kind, enhanced by his wide and deep knowledge of Latin literature and of the Greek Patristics. Kovalyns'kyj gives us evidence of Skovoroda's favorite books in the days when he taught in the College of Charkiv: "Plutarch, Philo Judaeus, Cicero, Horace, Lucian, Clement of Alexandria, Origen, Nile, Dionysius the Areopagite, Maximus the Confessor"[65].

Origen made the first attempt to transform (by Platonizing and Christianizing it) the Stoic individual hegemonic into an ability to grasp the invisible divine: Stoicism, as it was a naturalistic and monistic pantheism, could not conceive of an invisible dimension of the Absolute nor a special knowledge on the part of individual intimacy. Among the possible solutions opened by Origen to Christian Neoplatonism, that envisaged by Skovoroda differs both from the fully

62 H. Skovoroda, *Razgovor pjati putnikov o istinnom ščastii v žizni*, in Skovoroda 2011, p. 506.
63 Skovoroda 2011, p. 240.
64 von Ivánka 1964, pp. 79-80.
65 Kovalyns'kyj 2011, p. 1353.

mystical one (inaugurated by Evagrius of Pontus), and from Gregory of Nyssa's opposing one. By amending the Neoplatonism of his deification of the soul (with implied depersonalization), Gregory of Nyssa favored an Aristotelian epistemology and denied an autonomous intimate path towards God. Augustine, as we know, maintains firm the role of Grace and the ontological difference between creature and God, but, staying closer to the Neoplatonic sources, he is confident in the presence of an aspiration towards the divine. Criticizing those who seek God outside of themselves, he says, "they strive to go outside and leave their inner life, in whose intimacy there is God" (De Trinitate, VIII 7, 11). A subject on which Skovoroda's *Prolog* dwells at length, using one of his beloved biblical metaphors:

Blessed is the man who finds in his own home the source of consolation and does not chase the wind with Esau, hunting in the wild. Saul's daughter, Michal, who cast her glances out the window of her father's house, is the mother and tsarina of all those who wander about the wilderness following that dissolute tramp, who, having been met by our shepherd, is driven home like a wild beast. Where does the demon drive you? "Return to your house"[66].

It is a Personalism, religious and epistemological at the same time, so much Pauline as intellectualist in the Platonic and modern science sense. Skovoroda even professes the eternity of the world: "as long as there the apple tree, there also its shadow"[67]. An intellectualism that is not, however, free of mystical tension, with a clear proximity to monasticism and Evagrian Hesychasm, that in *Prolog* - his philosophical testament - Skovoroda wanted to emphasize: "Oh sea of my heart! Pure Abyss! Sacred source! I love you alone. I disappear in you and am transformed. Can you hear? This is what the fledgling eagle celebrates, the mother eagle's Theban wisdom"[68].

Even more than Augustine, Skovoroda's synthesis follows the method of the master of thought to which the Ukrainian philosopher was linked, i.e. Maximus the Confessor. Even for Skovoroda it can be said that his "genius lies in having hired himself five or six intellectual universes (...) and in having opened one on another."[69]

---

66 Skovoroda 2011, p. 231.
67 *Dialog. Imja emu: Potop zmiin*, in Skovoroda 2011, p. 953.
68 Skovoroda 2011, p. 232.
69 von Balthasar 2001, p. 49.

7. One of the peculiarities of *Narkiss* and his Prologue also lies in the fact that they represent a marked biographical significance in the life of an "integral" philosopher, which Skovoroda wanted to be, focusing, in the middle of the journey of his life, only on meditation and writing. This choice was not without pain, internal and external. His permanent abandonment of teaching took place in 1769 after a conflict with the bishop of Belgorod, who had prohibited the use of a treatise on ethics which he had composed; but in the past Skovoroda had had disagreements with the church authorities and suffered slanderous accusations from colleagues and ecclesiastics. His difficult relations with the surrounding environment caused him, as is natural, pain and anguish. In a letter of 1764, he describes a previous exclusion from Perejaslav's college (where he taught rhetoric) because of contrasts with the local bishop, "ejectus sum cum maximo dolore"[70]. In another letter of the same year he speaks in a heartfelt way of unjust accusations that had rained down on him from colleagues and ecclesiastics, defining him as a "corrupter of souls or heretic" and "Manichean"[71]. In the years which followed his decision to retire from teaching he suffered from attacks of anguish, and Skovoroda himself says in another letter that he had burned *A Symphony Called the Book of Askhan of Self-Knowledge*, one of his first philosophical dialogues, in a fit of rage. Related to these biographical data are also the "hypocrites" who are targeted in the second part of the *Prolog*; it is those who, in the name of common sense, reject both objective idealism and the mystical *indiamento*[72].

In this context, according to Natalia Pylypiuk, the dates of composition provide valuable clues to the reasons that led Skovoroda to write the dialogue; in her opinion, *Narkiss* was a kind of therapy to restore his inner equilibrium, while the *Prologue* was a sort of spiritual testament left to the new generations. Now, beyond the strictly biographical data, there was also a greater good at stake: namely the possibility of philosophy taken seriously and the entirety of philosophy as a synthesis of study and life. In the dedication of a philosophical dialogue shortly after *Narkiss*, Skovoroda had directly addressed his social condition, that of the first Ukrainian writer who devotes all

---

70 Letter to M. Kovalyns'kyj, spring 1764, in Skovoroda 2011, p. 1167.
71 Letter to Vasil' Maksymovyč, winter-spring 1764, in Skovoroda 2011, pp. 1266-1269.
72 Skovoroda 2011, p. 231.

his time to meditation and writing, without performing other social activities, "many wonder: what does Skovoroda do in his life? What does he do? (...) Joyful occupation (*zabava*), in Latin *oblectatio*, in Greek *diatribe*, in Slavic *glum*, is the summit, the climax, the flower and the seed of human life. (...) I practise the commandments of the Eternal. (...) In short: this is the diatribe and the rule of my life."[73] In short, Skovoroda remained faithful to the humanistic ideals learned at his *alma mater*, the Kyïvian Academy, where he took courses of rhetoric and poetics where the synthesis between *docere, delectare, movere* was exalted.

After his death, Skovoroda's teaching was not only appreciated by the Freemasonic circles: its influence is present both in the work of the "father" of Ukrainian prose, the journalist and writer Hryhorij Kvitka Osnov"janenko (who as a boy met Skovoroda and was later a friend of Gogol', influencing his work), and in those of Ivan Kotljarevs'kyj, the founder of modern Ukrainian literature. Even the birth in 1805 of the University of Charkiv - the first in Ukraine and where the romantic "rediscovery" of the Ukrainian culture and folklore took place - is linked to the figure of Skovoroda, because it was the local nobles, admirers of Skovoroda, who wanted to build the University, so much so that he became known as its "godfather". The writings of Skovoroda were also known to the writer and historian Ivan Kulžyns'kyj, Gogol's teacher in Nižyn high school. The Christology of Ševčenko and the theme of an existential choice in his poem *The Dream* is similar to Skovoroda's love for one's destiny[74]. It is, in every way, a cultural influence to be understood in a general sense; a full philosophical reception of Skovoroda had to wait until the second half of the 19th century.

However, what is most important is that the synthesis of Latin culture and humanism, modernism and Hesychasm spirituality that we find in the cultural and personal experience of Skovoroda is the highest point of the period of formation of the Ukrainian identity; a synthesis that the Baroque and pre-Romantic philosopher[75] bequeathed as a fruitful legacy for the history of Ukrainian contemporary culture.

---

73 H. Skovoroda, *Dialog, ili razglagol o drevnem mirě*, in Skovoroda 2011, p. 476.
74 Uškalov 2006.
75 Nachlik 1995.

BIBLIOGRAPHY

R. Arnou, *Le désir de Dieu dans la philosophie de Plotin*, Paris 1921.

H.H. Von Balthasar, *Massimo il Confessore. Liturgia Cosmica*, Milan 2001.

M.G. Bartolini "Poesia e filosofia nell'Ucraina del Settecento. Motivi epicurei nel *Sad božestvennych pesnej* di H.S. Skovoroda", in A. Costazza (ed.), *La poesia filosofica*, Milan 2007.

G. Bruno, *De gli eroici furori*, in G. Bruno, *Dialoghi filosofici italiani*, Milan 2000, pp. 755-960.

D. Čyževs'kyj, *Filosofija H.S. Skovorody*, Warsaw 1934.

E. von Erdmann, *Unähnliche Ähnlichkeit. Die Onto-Poetik des ukrainischen Philosophen Hryhorij Skovoroda (1722-1794)*, Köln-Weimar-Wien 2005.

R. Faggionato, *A Rosicrucian Utopia in Eighteenth-Century Russia: The Masonic Circle of N.I. Novikov*, Dordrecht 2005.

S. Frank, "Filosofskie otkliki: o nacionalizme v filosofii" ["Philosophical responses: nationalism in philosophy"], *Russkaja mysl'*, 1910, pp. 162-176.

A. Hippisley, "Introduction" to N. Maksimovich-Ambodik, *Emvlemy i simvoly (1788). The first Russian Emblem Book*, Leiden 1989.

J. Isajevyč, *Ukraïns'ke knyhovydannja. Vytoky, rozvytok, problemy* [*The Ukrainian Publishing; Origins, Development, Problems*], L'viv 2002.

E. von Ivánka, *Plato Christianus: Übernahme und Umgestaltung des Platonismus durch die Väter*, Einsiedeln 1964.

S. Jefremov, "Masonstvo v Ukraïni" ["Freemasonry in Ukraine"], Ï – *Nezaležnyj Kul'turolohičnyj Časopys*, 54, 2009, pp. 166-179 (ed. or. 1918).

M. Kašuba, "Traktuvannja Heorhijem Konys'kym problemy materiï" ["Heorhij Konys'kyj's interpretation of the problem of matter"], in V.M. Nyčyk (ed.), *Vid Vyšens'koho do Skovorody (z istoriï filosofs'koï dumky na Ukraïni XVI-XVIII st.)* [*From Vyšens'kyj to Skovoroda (A History of the XVI-XVIII-centuries Ukrainian Philosophical Thought)*], Kyïv 1972, pp. 96-102.

A. Koultchytskyi, "Skovoroda philosophe de la connaissance de soi-même et précurseur du personnalisme", in *Skovoroda philosophe ukrainien*, Paris 1976, pp. 55-110.

M. Kovalyns'kyj, *Žizn' Grigorija Skovorody* [*Life of Hryhorij Skovoroda*], in Skovoroda 2011, pp. 1343-1386.

V.M. Ničyk, *Kyevo-Mohyljans'ka Akademija ta nimec'ka kul'tura* [*The Mohylian Academy of Kyïv and German Culture*], Kyïv 2001.

A. Niženec', *Na zlami dvoch svitiv. Rosvidka pro H.S. Skovorodu i charkivs'hyj kolehium* [*At the Turn of Two Worlds. Research about H.S. Skovoroda and the Charkiv College*], Charkiv 1970.

N. Ordine, *La soglia dell'ombra. Letteratura, filosofia e pittura in Giordano Bruno*, Venice 2003.

J. Nachlik, "Hryhorij Skovoroda jak poet-preromantyk", *Zapysky Naukovoho Tovarystva im. Ševčenka. Praci filolohičnoï sekciï*, 229, 1995, pp. 29-45.

M. Praz, *Studies in Seventeenth Century Imagery*, Rome 1975[2].

R. Pič, "Skovorodynivs'kyj mif pro Narkisa v svitli romantyčnoï koncepciï mifotvorčosti" ["The Skovorodian Myth of Narcissus in the Light of the Romantic Conception of the Myth"], *Sučasnist'*, 1995, 10, pp. 161-167.

N. Pylypiuk, "The Primary Door: At the Threshold of Skovoroda's Theology and Poetics", *Harvard Ukrainian Studies*, 1990, 3/4, pp. 551-583.

N. Pylypiuk, "Skovoroda's Divine Narcissism", *Journal of Ukrainian Studies*, 1-2, 1997, pp. 13-50.

S. Ricci, *La fortuna del pensiero di Giordano Bruno. 1650-1750*, Florence 1990.

S.P. Scherer, "The Narcissus: Skovoroda's «First-Born Son»", *Journal of Ukrainian Studies*, 1-2, 1997, pp. 51-64.

S.P. Scherer, "Enlightment Elements in the Tought of Hryhorij Skovoroda", *Michigan Academician*, 38, 2008, pp. 61-77.

H. Skovoroda, *Povne zibrannja tvoriv u dvoch tomach* [*Complete Works in Two Volumes*], vol. I, Kyïv 1973.

H. Skovoroda, *Povna akademična zbirka tvoriv* [*Academic Edition of Complete Works*], L. Uškalov (ed.), Charkiv-Edmonton-Toronto 2011.

N. Sumcov, "Predislovie a Žitie Skovorody, opisannoe drugom ego, M.I. Kovalinskim" ["Preface to *Life of Skovoroda*, wrote by a friend of his, M.I. Kovalinskij"], *Kievskaja Starina*, 1886, XVI, pp. 106-107.

Symbola et Emblemata Jussu atque aspiciis Petri Alexeidis, Amsterdam 1705.

A. Uguccioni, "L'iconografia di Narciso nel "Roman de la Rose", esempio di amore cortese", in R. Varese (ed.), *Studi per Pietro Zampetti*, Ancona 1993, pp. 71-75.

L. Uškalov, *Z istoriï ukraïns'koï literatury XVII-XVIII stolit'* [*On the History of XVII-XVIII-centuries Ukrainian Literature*], Charkiv 1999.

L. Uškalov, *Hryhorij Skovoroda: seminarij* [*Hryhorij Skovoroda: A Seminar*], Charkiv 2004.

L. Uškalov, *Eseï pro ukraïns'ke baroko* [*Essays on the Ukrainian Baroque*], Kyïv 2006.

L. Uškalov, "Hryhorij Skovoroda", in Skovoroda 2011, pp. 9-48.

F. Yates, *Giordano Bruno and the Hermetic Tradition*, London 1964.

T. Zakydalsky, "Skovoroda's Moral Philosophy", in R.H. Marshall, T.E. Bird (eds.), *Hryhoryj Savyč Skovoroda. An Anthology of Critical Articles*, Edmonton-Toronto 1994, pp. 239-250.

4. Poland in the Humanistic Historiosophy of Taras Ševčenko

The French original of this essay will be published in 2015 in the Proceedings of the study day on Ševčenko (on the bicentenary of his birth) organized by Inalco (Institut National des Langues et Civilisations Orientales) of Paris, Sorbonne Paris Cité Université.

1. The historical dimension is of vital importance in European literary Romanticism. Similarly, history is a major issue of Ševčenko's poetry, which often takes the form of a "historiosophy"[1] or a meta-history[2]. The relationship with Poland cannot, therefore, fail to be a privileged question in the works of the Ukrainian *kobzar*. Since the fourteenth century, when the Polish King Casimir the Great invaded Galicia and conquered it after a twenty-year war, relations between Ukraine and Poland have always been very close, but long marked by hostility rather than by friendship. It was above all a social conflict: the Lublin Union of 1569 having handed over to Poland all Ukrainian lands, the kings of Rzeczpospolita had donated to the Polish *szlachta* (nobility) immense areas in the Ukrainian "vacant" spaces, allowing the creation of vast dominions and ban lands. Thus, the Ukrainian peasants fell under what has been called the second serfdom[3], a severe form of social domination that lasted until 1861-1863. The great Cossack revolt of Bohdan Chmel'nyc'kyj in 1648 was fueled by social resentment on the part of the peasants for this aristocratic domination, but also by religious and national hostility due to the introduction in Ukraine of the United Church (or Uniate).

---

1 Barabaš 2004; Jaremenko, 2007.
2 Grabowicz 1982, pp. 17-43.
3 Kamiński 1975.

The *Hajdamaky* or bands of Cossacks and rebellious peasants of the eighteenth century, glorified by Ševčenko in his homonymous epic poem of 1841, continued this anti-noble and anti-Polish struggle until the Russian annexation of the Right Bank of the Dnipro (1772-1795). With the legal leveling between the Polish aristocracy and the Russian nobility, declared in 1793 by Empress Catherine II, the eleven thousand families of Polish landowners (of which two hundred possessed at least a thousand servants) always maintained economic and social primacy in Ukraine on the Right Bank, until 1920[4].

On the Left Bank, a similar phenomenon led the upper classes of the Cossacks (the *staršyna*) to ennoble itself by governing the autonomous Cossack state (Hetmanate), born after the revolt of 1648 and abolished in 1765; an ennoblement recognized by Catherine II, who decided in 1785 to incorporate the Cossack nobility into the *dvorjanstvo,* or Russian imperial nobility. But the Heraldry Commission of St. Petersburg, which slowed up the procedures for the recognition of the noble title, did not grant all the requests.

2. The main, but not the only source[5] of Ševčenko's knowledge of the historical past of Ukraine was the *History of the Rus'* (*Istorija Rusov*), which is the principal expression of Ukrainian and Russian pre-romanticism. It was an anonymous manuscript, written in Russian, the introduction of which presented it as a Ukrainian chronicle, written over the centuries by a group of Orthodox monks and published in 1760 by Heorhij Konys'kyj, one of the most prestigious professors of the Academy of Kyïv; Ševčenko also called the manuscript the "chronicle of Konys'kyj". Indeed, the *Istorija Rusov* had been written by an early nineteenth century Ukrainian compiler who had used various Cossack chronicles, mixing them with free literary interpolations. This text, which was also a syncretic fusion between the Enlightenment ideals of freedom and the Romantic taste for manipulation and historical narrations[6], was very successful and circulated in manuscript form before being published in 1846.

The *Istorija* expressed the positions of the Ukrainian elites at the end of the Napoleonic Wars; these elites felt threatened by difficulties

---

4 Social relations in Ukraine between the nineteenth century's Polish uprisings are analyzed by Beauvois 1991.
5 Kulikova 2011.
6 Plokhy 2012.

with the imperial nobility and by the cooperation of the Polish magnates with the Tsarist regime (which, however, was weakened during Napoleon's time and ended with the uprising of 1830)[7]. The *Istorija* stated a common origin for the "two" Russians peoples, the Great and Little Russians (i.e., Russians and Ukrainians) and claimed for the latter birthright in the historical foundation of the ancient kyïvian Rus'. Therefore, the use of the word "Ukraine" was rejected, judged to be of Polish origin and which, according to the anonymous compiler (or the anonymous compilers), was intended to divide the two Russian peoples. Above all the epic struggle of the Cossacks against the Poles was exalted, emphasizing in particular the ancient Cossack freedom that the Tsars had agreed to preserve.

The first to be interested in the work were the progressive Russian poets, such as the Decembrist Ryleev and Alexandr Puškin. The *Istorija Rusov* also exerted a strong influence on Gogol': many episodes of *Taras Bul'ba* have the famous manuscript as a source[8]. Ševčenko was also fascinated by *Istorija*; according to Mychajlo Drahomanov, "between 1840 and 1844 he studied the *Istorija Rusov* [...]; in the years 1844-1845 no work, except the Bible, had a comparable influence on his spiritual development"[9]. But Ševčenko's reading of the "Chronicle" was very different from Gogol's and from that of the author of the compilation. Gogol' did not really believe in the rebirth of the Cossack nation: its overall concept seemed to want to make his art the model of an imperial culture that transcended the boundaries of Russian nationalism, embodied by Puškin[10]. Ševčenko wanted to be, on the contrary, the champion of the revival of the Cossacks and the Ukrainian nation, subjugated by Russian imperial domination; in fact, one of the themes of his philosophy of history is the flogging of Ukrainian servility and "collaboration" with Russian domination. What set Ševčenko apart from the *Istorija Rusov* and Gogol' was also a non-hostile attitude, on the part of the Ukrainian *kobzar*, towards the Polish nation.

---

7 On the phenomenon of temporary cooperation of Polish magnates with the Tsarist regime, see: Beauvois 2003.
8 Plokhy 2012, pp. 15-27; 51-60.
9 Drahomanov 1879, p. 147.
10 Bojanowska 2009.

3. Ševčenko's very original vision (compared to the "Little Russian" ideology or the ideas of "Ucrainophiles" of the second half of the nineteenth century), of Ukrainian-Polish relations can be attributed to biographical, cultural and ideal reasons. From a personal perspective, Bronisław Zaleski (the best friend of the Ukrainian poet during his exile in Orenburg) says in his memoirs that "Ševčenko spoke good Polish (...), but did not dare write in Polish. I have always written to him in Polish, and he answered me in his language, half Russian and half Little-Russian"[11].

Ševčenko had lived until the age of 14 in Right Bank Ukraine where the presence of the Polish language was widespread and socially important. The influence of Ukrainian culture had given, in any case, a distinct look to this part of the Polish universe, thanks to economic, inter-ethnic, cultural and administrative exchanges. So that, while some Ukrainians used Polish as a culturally and socially prestigious medium of expression, it succumbed to foreign influences and was like a dialect. In particular, the less affluent spheres of the Polish population were imbued with Ukrainian sensitivity and folk culture.[12] On the other hand, Polish was the language most used in the administration and in the tribunals of the three Ukrainian provinces of the Russian Empire; not only the *szlachta*, but many administrators of the cities and part of the Orthodox rural clergy spoke Polish. However, national divisions remained significant and a real fusion of different cultures and different identities was still very distant.

Ševčenko was a servant of the Engelhard family, who owned 50,000 souls in different provinces of the Empire. Taras was serving as valet *(kozačok)* in his owners' house (they were of Baltic-German origin, but partly Polonized), where both Russian and Polish were spoken[13]. In 1823, Ševčenko's sister, Kateryna, married the peasant Anton Krasyc'kyj, whose name suggests a Polish origin. Subsequently, from the autumn of 1828 until the beginning of 1831, following his master Pavel Engelhard, Ševčenko lived in Vilnius, a city in which the presence of the Poles was even more pronounced than in the Right Bank; in Vilnius, he fell in love with a Polish girl, Jadwiga Gusikowska, who worked as a seamstress. The two lovers communi-

---

11 Franko 1890, p. 31.
12 Beauvois 1991, pp. 125-130.
13 Lebedincev 1882.

cated in Polish[14]. In Vilnius, the young Taras witnessed the Polish uprising of 1830 against the Tsarist regime, an event full of political significance and romantic libertarianism, which no doubt impressed the future cantor of the liberation of Ukraine.

Ševčenko's personal contacts with friends of Polish nationality continued throughout his life. In Vilnius he moved in the circles of those who attended the university courses in drawing and painting held by Professor Jan Rustem, where there were many young Poles, who also kept alive the memory of Joachim Lelewel's history lessons, the famous Polish historian and patriot, cited by Ševčenko in the autobiographical novel *The Artist* (1856). In the same text, the author presents a good Polish friend, who in the novel is called Leonard Demski. Ševčenko tells of political discussions and exciting cultural conversations between them in St. Petersburg, but Leonard died early of tuberculosis and his funeral was paid for by Taras. In the student and cultural circles of the Imperial capital, Ševčenko kept company with many Poles: with his colleague, the Polish P. Żukowski, he illustrated two books of the Russian historian Nikolaj Polevoj while befriending (thanks to the brothers Żukowski)[15], Romuald Podbereski, a Pole from Vilnius, who was the director of the Petersburg literary magazine "Rocznik Literacki" (in Polish); and with Jan Barszczewski, a Polish-Belarusian writer who published in the imperial capital the almanac "Niezabudka" (1840-1845). Podbereski's praise for Ševčenko in 1844 in the magazine "Tygodnik Petersburski" (the "official" Polish culture review of the time, close to the Russian government) is very interesting; Ševčenko there is termed as a "philosopher, poet, artist" and his *Hajdamaky* is celebrated as a great poem[16].

During his exile beyond the Urals, which lasted more than ten years, Ševčenko met several Poles, who like him were forcibly recruited in their thousands in the Russian army stationed in Asia. The researchers listed at least 40 Polish patriots with whom he had friendly relations. The closest was Bronisław Zaleski, who Ševčenko called in a letter of 1856, "my only friend"[17]. Bronisław was a relative of Józef Bogdan Zaleski, one of the representatives of the school called "Ukrainian" of Polish literature; he helped Ševčenko

14 Čalyj 1862, p. 52.
15 Verves 1964, p. 17.
16 *Ibid.*, p. 24.
17 *Lysty do T.H. Ševčenka* 1962, p. 104.

to learn more about Polish literature and then, during his exile in France, helped to make the Ukrainian poet known among the Polish emigrants.

4. It is true that Drahomanov reports two testimonies of that time to support his idea that "Ševčenko maintained until the end distrust and hostility towards foreigners, towards the neighbors of Ukraine"[18]; the first is that of Jakob Gordon (he cites hearsay), who actually stated that "Ševčenko did not like the Poles, and he could not stand the Muscovites"[19]; but Jakob Gordon (aka Maximilian Jatowt) firmly stated that Ševčenko was a "red", which prompts us to think that his knowledge of the Ukrainian poet was superficial. We must also consider that in the 1850s and 1860s, Ukrainian-Polish relations had become colder due to some hostility towards Polishness by the new generation of "Ucrainophiles", subsequently reinforced by the indifference manifested by the Ukrainian masses during the Polish uprising of 1863. So much so that the son of Mickiewicz, Ladislas, from his exile in Paris thundered against "the Russophiles (...), men with no luck, false spirits and mediocre scholars, who attack the Polish nobility [through] collections of poems, such as *Kobzar*, *Hajdamaki*, *Chata*". He also spoke of the "destructive communism" of the magazine *Osnova* (!) directed by Kostomarov[20].

In this misinterpretation of Ševčenko's work, a key role was played by the fact that in Russian editions of *Hajdamaky*, those usually read by the Poles, the Introduction written by Ševčenko was absent[21]; here he had greatly attenuated the anti-Polish hostility that the title and the theme of the poem could imply. This negative attitude towards the works of Ševčenko by a part of the Polish emigrées in Paris had encouraged Bronisław Zaleski (also a refugee in Paris) to engage in an unlikely defense of his Ukrainian friend, which led him to affirm: "Ševčenko told me one day that his *Hajdamaky*, and all of this orientation, caused him pain"[22]. On the other hand, an example of this coldness in relations between Poles and Ukrainophiles is the frank statement that Kulyš addressed to Ševčenko in 1858, in which he crit-

---

18 Drahomanov 1879, p. 152.
19 Gordon 1864, p. 163.
20 Cited in Beauvois 1993, p. 87.
21 Kravčenko 2008, p. 386.
22 Franko 1890, p. 45.

icized the poem *To the Poles* (where Ševčenko expressed his doctrine of Slavic brotherhood between the two peoples) that the author had sent him in manuscript[23].

The second testimony invoked by Drahomanov is by Aleksandr Afanas'ev-Čužbinskij, according to which "Ševčenko did not like the Poles"; a testimony, however, immediately followed by the rather contradictory statement: "he was attracted to Mickiewicz, whom he repeatedly tried to translate"[24]. Despite their limitations, it can be assumed that the meaning of these testimonies resides in that typical ambivalence that universally characterizes the identity-estrangement relationship, increased by the complexity of Ševčenko's personality[25]. However, we cannot doubt Ševčenko's positive attitudes towards Polishness, considering the mass of objective data that contradict the statements of Drahomanov mentioned above.

A special figure, among those forcibly recruited Poles who had fraternized with Ševčenko, was that of the young Zygmunt Sierakowski (1827-1863), a patriot and native of Volhynia, who was animated by a strong force of spirit and great humanity; thanks to his abilities, at the end of the period of forced exile he was able to make a career in the Russian army, becoming at the same time one of the exponents of the cultural life of St. Petersburg; he fought to improve the living conditions of ordinary soldiers, for the linguistic autonomy of Ukraine and had contacts with Garibaldi and Herzen. He was hanged at the end of the uprising of 1863, of which he had been one of the leaders in Vilnius[26]. In his letters to Ševčenko, he called him affectionately *bat'ko* (father). Sierakowski had worked closely with Countess Tolstoj to get permission for Ševčenko to be able to stay in St. Petersburg after the end of his banishment. During his last years in St. Petersburg, in the circle of friends that surrounded Ševčenko, there were still a great deal of patriots and Polish intellectuals.

5. The positive attitude and sense of brotherhood that Ševčenko harbored toward the Poles, according to most commentators, was especially evident during the period of his exile, or appears in connec-

---

23 *Lysty do T.H. Ševčenka* 1962, p. 124.
24 Čužbinskij 1861, p. 12.
25 Grabowicz 1982, pp. 1-16.
26 Usenko 2013.

tion with the slavophilism of the Brotherhood of Saints Cyril and Methodius (the membership of which caused Ševčenko to be exiled); but those who have studied this issue carefully, as did Hryhorij Verves, have revealed the anterior origin of this attitude[27]. Verves noted that the first expression of a Polish-Ukrainian pan-Slavism is already present in *Hajdamaky*, where Ševčenko says, referring to the clashes between Ukrainians and Poles, "and why do people die? With the same father, children equal./Better to live and fraternize"[28].

Now, we do not know much about Ševčenko's readings in the years spent in Vilnius and in the first period of his stay in St. Petersburg, but most researchers are confident that he had a knowledge of Polish literature, especially the works of Mickiewicz, Lelewel and the writers of the so-called «Ukrainian school» such as Zaleski, Goszczyński and, above all, Michał Czajkowski, a legendary soldier and writer figure who, in 1837, published his *Cossack Stories*. Czajkowski's father was Polish and he was descended, on mother's side, from a former Cossack hetman; he dreamed of the restoration of the Hetmanate within a pan-Slavic confederation, with Kyïv as capital. There was also an example of what can be called Mickiewicz's "national internationalism"[29] which envisioned the restoration of the autonomy of all Slavic peoples and the reconstitution of the Polish Rzeczpospolita. Knowledge of these works, the positive reception of his poems by the Polish magazines of Saint Petersburg, the Ukrainophilism of some members of Polish culture, the self-critical positions (anti-magnate and anti-uniatism) of some Polish historians (such as Lelewel), are all factors that, associated with Ševčenko's personal familiarity with Polishness, explain his slavophilism which was well disposed towards Poland.

Shortly after the quoted verse, the *Hajdamaky* explains the key to understanding Ševčenko's philosophy of history concerning the Ukrainian-Polish conflict, a key that remained constant in his poetic works: "the children of ancient Slavs,/are drunk with blood./But who is the culprit? The priests (*ks'ondzy*) and the Jesuits"[30]. The author

---

27 Verves 1964, p. 31. For a brief and lively presentation of the figure of Verves as educator and Slavist, see: Paščenko, 2013
28 Ševčenko 2014, p. 80.
29 Nowak 2005, pp. 261-3.
30 Ševčenko 2014, pp. 80-81. In the Ukrainian language, the word *ks'ondzy* indicates Catholic priests.

himself affixed a note to the last verse: "Before Union, the Cossacks and the Poles lived in peace, and had it not been for the Jesuits, maybe they would not have massacred each other; it was the papal legate, the Jesuit Possevino, who introduced the Union into Ukraine"[31]. So, unlike almost all other Ukrainian Romantic writers and, especially, the next generation of Ukrainophiles, and also Hruševs'kyj (who was a student of Antonovyč, the leader of the Ukrainophiles) and Franko, in Ševčenko there is no acrimony toward the Polish world; certainly, rather than a position of scientific historiography, here we have an attitude based on moral values. In the *Preface* to *Hajdamaky*, the cultural and political program of Ševčenko is even more explicit:

Thank God it is the past - and this is even more true when we remember that we are children of the same mother, we are all Slavs. The heart hurts, but you have to tell it: so that the children and grandchildren will see how wrong their fathers were, so that they may fraternize again with their enemies, and the Slav lands be covered with wheat, like gold, with no borders, from sea to sea[32].

This preface was omitted in the Russian editions of the poem, which explains - as we said - why many Poles were not aware of Ševčenko's true positions.

The culmination of Ševčenko's vision of the Polish-Ukrainian relationship is the poem *To the Poles*, written in the first months of exile (1847). Here, he repeats the image of an idyllic past of fraternity, broken by the intrigues of priests, "who burned our quiet paradise." A description of the pain and the blood then follows. Then there is the final part of the poem: "Then, Polish, friend, brother/never satisfied, priests, magnates/have made us strangers, have separated us,/ and we would live, even now, as before./Extend the hand to the Cossack/and tender a pure heart./Once again, in the name of Christ /we will renew our haven of tranquility"[33]. It is a program of brotherhood and friendship that seemed completely out of place in those years, but that proved prophetic.

From the historical point of view, critics who pointed out (as did Ivan Franko) the non-existence of such idyllic relations between Poles and Ukrainians before the Union of Brest (1596) had good reason to

---

31 *Ibid.*, p. 126.
32 *Ibid.*, p. 130.
33 Ševčenko 2003, v. 2, p. 581. The first Russian edition of this poem appeared in 1867, devoid of the last eight verses, which the censor obviously did not like; see: pp. 582-583.

do so; although the Ruthenian nobles of Volhynia and Kyïv had obtained, at the time of the enlargement of Polish domination in the central regions of Ukraine, guarantees for their rights and privileges[34], there were deeper reasons of contrast, already mentioned, between the Polish colonizers and the Ukrainian masses. There were then, in Rzeczpospolita, prejudice and hostility towards the Ruthenian and Orthodox nobility: for example, the Orthodox bishops were not members of the Senate, unlike the Catholics; on the other hand, even the Uniate bishops never obtained this privilege.

But it would be wrong to judge Ševčenko's philosophy of history according to the accuracy of documents: Ševčenko's history is meta-ethical and meta-political, based on humanistic ideals. It is a programmatic philosophy of history, which looks to the present (thus a persecuted Poland) and to the future rather than to the past.

6. In parallel to biographical and cultural data, Ševčenko's polonophilism was fuelled especially by ideal motivations. Despite the presence in his work of some national stereotypes (like the "stingy" Jew and the Germanness of Catherine II), guilty enemies (the Jesuits or the Muscovites in their excess of power) and some victimizations, Ševčenko's poetry, as indicated by Grabowicz, "is remarkably free of an ethnic or group bias"[35]. Even more, in his private life he was always surrounded by cosmopolitan circles of friends, which included Russians, Poles, Germans, etc. We know, finally, that he signed the letter of collective protest (with Vovčok, Kostomarov, Kulyš and Nomys) against anti-Semitism, addressed to *Russkij Vestnik*[36].

The philosophical humanism of Ševčenko is classical-biblical and one of its sources is the teaching (which deserves to be better known) that he received at the Imperial Academy of Fine Arts. Vasyl' Jaremenko stressed that the quotes from historians (Herodotus, Livy, Plutarch, but also Vasari, Champollion, Gibbon, etc.) contained in his narrative works in Russian, written in exile and without being able to consult sources, reveal the deep humanism absorbed by Ševčenko in the Academy of St. Petersburg[37]. Moreover, Ševčenko tells us

---

34 The privileges granted by King Sigismund II Augustus to the Ruthenian nobility, through the Union of Lublin, are collected in *Akta Unji* 1932, p. 305, p. 316.
35 Grabowicz 1993, p. 305.
36 Ševčenko 2003, v. 6, pp. 222-223.
37 Jaremenko 2007, p. 175.

in *The Artist*, that Karl Brjullov asked his students to use Biblical and Greek-Roman subjects for the artist's proofs. Classicism, it must be remembered, which had arrived in Russia a century earlier with the clergy of the Academy of Kyïv, called by Peter I to found the Russian Academies[38].

In the formation of the humanistic philosophy of history of Ševčenko, even his contacts with the Decembrists played a role. Indeed, Ševčenko had attended Decembrist circles, which did much for his liberation from serfdom, while the vice-president of the Academy of Fine Arts, Count Fëodor Petrovič Tolstoj, was a Decembrist; some works of Ševčenko (*Neophytes*, for example) are devoted to them, others (like *The Dream*) are full of Decembrist symbolism[39].

These liberal and classicist ideals have been reworked in his humanist philosophy of history, which condenses the universalism professed by Ševčenko. It is a universalism that leads to a millenarian hope of brotherhood among peoples which, in addition to being close to the positions of Mickiewicz, is very similar to the ideals of Giuseppe Mazzini[40].

---

38 Kortschmaryk 1976.
39 Latyš 2014, pp. 37-50.
40 On Mazzini's millenarianism: De Giorgi 2010, pp. 67-74.

Akta Unji Polski z Litwą, 1385-1791 [*Acts of the Polish-Lithuanian Union, 1385-1791*], Crakow 1932.

J. Barabaš, "Istoriosofija Tarasa Ševčenka" ["Ševčenko's Historiosophy"], *Slovo i Čas*, 2004, 3, pp. 15-37.

D. Beauvois, *Le noble, le serf et le révizor. La noblesse polonaise entre le tsarisme et les masses ukrainiennes (1831-1863)*, Paris, 1991.

D. Beauvois, *La bataille de la terre en Ukraine, 1863-1914. Les Polonais et les conflits socio-ethniques*, Lille, 1993.

D. Beauvois, *Pouvoir russe et noblesse polonaise en Ukraine. 1793-1830*, Paris 2003.

E. Bojanowska, "Equivocal Praise and National Imperial Conundrums: Gogol's *A Few Words about Pushkin*", *Canadian Slavonic Papers*, 2009, 2-3, pp. 173-196.

S. Čalyj, "Materialy dlja biografii T.G. Ševčenko" ["Materials for T.G. Ševčenko's Biography"], *Osnova*, 1862, 5, pp. 45-62.

A. Čužbinskij, "Vospominanija o T.G. Ševčenke" ["Remembrances of T.G. Ševčenko"], *Russkoe Slovo*, May 1861, pp. 1-39.

F. De Giorgi, *Millenarismo educatore. Mito gioachimita e pedagogia civile in Italia dal Risorgimento al fascismo*, Rome 2010.

M. Drahomanov, "Ševčenko, ukraïnofily i socializm" ["Ševčenko, the Ukrainophiles and Socialism"], *Hromada*, IV, 1879, pp. 101-230.

I. Franko, (ed.), *Lystočky do vinka na mohylu Ševčenka v XIX rokovyny joho smerti* [*Leaves for the Wreath on the Tomb of Ševčenko in the Nineteenth Anniversary of his Death*], L'viv 1890.

J. Gordon, *Sołdat: nowe pamiętniki* [*Soldier: New Memoirs*], Bruxelles-Leipzig 1864.

G.G. Grabowicz, *The Poet as Mythmaker. A Study of Symbolic Meaning in Taras Ševčenko*, Cambridge (Mass.) 1982.

G.G. Grabowicz, "Insight and Blindness in the Reception of Ševčenko: The Case of Kostomarov", *Harvard Ukrainian Studies*, 1993, 1-2, pp. 279-340.

V.I. Jaremenko, "Do problemy istoriosofiï Tarasa Ševčenka: metodolohični pidchody" ["The Problem of Taras Shevchenko's Historiosophy: Methodological Approaches"], *Slovo i Čas*, 2007, 3, pp. 19-27.

V.I. Jaremenko, "Svitova istorija u tvorčij spadščyni Tarasa Ševčenka: sproba istoriosofs'koho pročytannja" ["World History in the Creative Legacy of Taras Ševčenko: A Historiosophical Reading Attempt"], *Ukraïns'kyj istoryčnyj žurnal*, 5, 2007, pp. 174-188.

A. Kamiński, "Neo-Serfdom in Poland-Lithuania", *Slavic Review*, 34, 2, 1975, pp. 253-268.

F.B. Kortschmaryk, *The Kievan Academy and its Role in the Organization of Education in Russia at the Turn of the Seventeenth Century*, New York 1976.

S. Kravčenko, "Pol's'ka publicystyka 20-x-30-x rokiv XX st. pro tvorčist' Tarasa Ševčenka" ["Polish Publications of 20s-30s of the Twentieth Century on the Works of Taras Ševčenko"], *Volyn' Filolohična: Tekst i Kontekst*, 6-1, 2008, pp. 366-373.

O.V. Kulikova, "Tradyciï ukraïns'koï barokovoï istoriohrafiï u rannij tvorčosti Tarasa Ševčenka" ["The Ukrainian Baroque Historiographical Tradition in the Early Works of Taras Ševčenko"], *Visnyk Charkivs'koho nacional'noho universytetu – Filosofia*, 936, 61, 2011, pp. 176-180.

J. Latyš, *Dekabrysty v Ukraïni. Istoriohrafični studiï* [*The Decembrists in Ukraine. Historiographical Study*], Kyïv 2014.

P. Lebedincev, "Taras Grigor'jevič Ševčenko", *Kievskaja starina*, September 1882, pp. 560-567.

Lysty do T.H. Ševčenka. 1840-1861 [*Letters to T.H. Ševčenko. 1840-1861*], Kyïv 1962.

L. Mickiewicz, *La Pologne et ses provinces méridionales*, Paris 1869.

A. Nowak, "Between Imperial Temptation and Anti-Imperial Function in Eastern European Politics: Poland from the Eighteenth to Twenty-First Century", *Slavic Euroasian Studies*, 7, 2005, pp. 247-284.

J. Paščenko, "Slavistyka, jakoï nema: Hryhorij Davydovyč Verves" ["Slavic Studies that There are Not: Hryhorij Davydovyč Verves"], *Narodoznavči zošyty*, 6, 2013, pp. 1169-1172.

S. Plokhy, *The Cossack Myth. History and Nationhood in the Age of Empires*, Cambridge 2012.

T. Ševčenko, *Zibrannja tvoriv* [*Collected Works*], t. 2, *Poesija 1847-1861*, Kyïv 2003.

T. Ševčenko, *Zibrannja tvoriv* [*Collected Works*], t. 6, Kyïv 2003.

T. Ševčenko, *Hajdamaky (faksymile vydannja 1841 roku)* [*Hajdamaky (Facsimile of the 1841 Edition)*], Kyïv 2014.

P.H. Usenko, "Žyttjevyj podvyh Zygmunta Serakovs'koho (do 150-riččja povstannja 1863 r.)" ["The Heroic Life of Zygmunt Sierakowski (On the 150th Anniversary of the Uprising of 1863)"], *Ukraïns'kyj istoryčnyj žurnal*, 2013, 5, pp. 110-116.

H.D. Verves, *Ševčenko i Pol'šča* [*Ševčenko and Poland*], Kyïv 1964.

5. CROSS IDENTITY OF A METAPHYSICIAN OF SENSUALITY: JAROSŁAW IWASZKIEWICZ

The work began as a contribution to the Conference "Borders", organized by the Lincoln University of Pennsylvania (USA) in April of 2014 and was later published in the 2nd issue of "The Lincoln Humanities Journal", in the autumn of 2014.

1. In 1917 more than a million of Poles lived in Ukraine and Belarus, two countries that were part of the Russian Empire. The presence of so many Poles was due to the fact that some Ukrainian regions (Volhynia, Podolia, Kyïv region, etc.) were previously part of the Commonwealth of Poland and Lithuania. With the Partitions of the Polish–Lithuanian Commonwealth (1772-1795) conducted by Russia, Prussia and Austria, a large part of present Ukraine became a province of the Russian Empire.

Many Poles of Ukraine were members of the more affluent Ukrainian social classes, since the Tsarist regime had maintained - even after the Partitions - the dominant economic role that the Poles had, to keep order in new provinces and to better exploit the Ukrainian agricultural production. In 1904 the Poles possessed 46% of the land of the Central-Western Ukraine (Dnieper Right Bank) and 54% of its industrial production (especially sugar); land ownership was concentrated in large estates owned by a few magnate families. Between the magnates and the remainder of the Polish population there were large economic and social differences. But a psychological affinity was evident for all the Poles of the Kresy (Borders, as in Poland were named the Ukrainian lands inhabited by the Poles). We must in fact consider that almost all the Ukrainian Poles could boast of a title of nobility, and they all were the descendants of ancient colonizers.

After the Russian Revolution and World War I, a large number of Poles left Ukraine (one million throughout the former Tsarist Empire) and fled to the new Polish state; consequently, the number of Poles remaining in Dnieper Ukraine decreased by more than one-third, from 685,000 in 1909 to 410,000 in 1926. Among the Polish emigrants there were many landowners and all the nationalists (the members of the National Democratic Party), who felt, above all, citizens of the reborn Polish state. Another group of emigrants, that left Ukraine to settle in Poland, was formed by urban low or middle-classes, intellectuals or professionals, who despite being romantically linked to the Ukrainian land, had no concrete reasons for staying in Ukraine but hoped to have a better life in Poland; one of them was the young writer Jarosław Iwaszkiewicz, who in 1917 was 23 years old.

Like many others Ukrainian Poles, Iwaszkiewicz was not particularly restrained in an independent or Bolshevik Ukraine; in both cases, the fate of the Poles did not seem to be bright: the Ukrainian patriots did not like the Poles, as old colonizer, while the Poles came to be classified as "enemy nation" in the Stalinist regime[1]. Iwaszkiewicz justified his choice to abandon Ukraine and leave for Warsaw in October 1918 (aided by August Iwański jr, a relative of his rich and aristocratic) as follows: "Many signs, between sky and earth, announced me that I hadn't more reasons to stay in Kijów (…); without sorrow I left Ukraine that was dead or dying". Anyway, it wasn't an easy departure and the souvenir of Ukraine, which was still their homeland, longing gripped all the rest of their lives. In fact, Iwaszkiewicz adds: "in those new places I felt tight, compared to the wide plains of my childhood"[2].

2. Iwaszkiewicz's training there was in the high schools of the region of Jelysavethrad (a southwestern Ukrainian city a few hundred kilometers from Kyïv, renamed Kirovograd by Stalin in 1939) and then at the Conservatory and the University of Kyïv. His father participated in the failed uprising that Poles tried in 1863 against the Russian Tsarist power; at the time when Jarosław was born, his father had a modest job as an accountant in a sugar factory owned by a Polish magnate. Although the social status of his family was so very different, Jarosław knew the Polish aristocracy's world very well: his mother had been received as a child and raised in the home of

---

1 Morris 2004.
2 Iwaszkiewicz 2010, p. 157.

the Baron Taube, her distant relative. Taube's grandson, Karol Szymanowski, also a noble and older than Jarosław, would become the most influential personality in the training of the young writer. In the noble Polish families of Ukraine Jarosław also worked as a tutor. The distance between the magnates and the rest of the Polish community of Ukraine never wavered, a gap not only social but also psychological, as Iwaszkiewicz resolutely affirmed himself: "It was not possible to compare the two worlds as this caste was separated by a deep chiasm from the world to which I belonged"[3]. But the traits of the aristocratic world remained in young Jarosław, with a strong love for beauty and aloof behavior, which later earned him some accusations of snobbery.

In the first pages of his main work, the epic novel in three volumes - published in the Fifties - *Sława i Chwała* [*Glory and Vainglory*], Iwaszkiewicz depicted one of the last moments of the youth and refined aristocratic life he shared with Szymanowski's family and with other Polish aristocratic families in which he worked as a tutor: in a seaside villa, Paulina Szyller and her son, the composer Edgar (character inspired by Karol Szymanowski) hosted in the days of July 1914 Ewelina Royska, wife of a landowner from Podolia, her young son Józio with his tutor Kazimierz Spychała; the young singer Eliżbeta Szyller just returned from Vienna. After she freshened up, and before going to sleep, Eliżbeta was invited to sing *Verborgenheit* (H. Wolf):

With the first note, sung in a low voice, a smile in which mingled joy and embarrassment settled on the lips of Eliżbeta. The first E flat seemed to be produced from the bow of a cello and Edgar gave his sister a look of admiration, almost surprised. Lady Royska and Lady Szyller were at the height of bliss. Spychała felt that something unspeakable was happening and lowered his head. (...) Without making a sound, so that no one - except Royska - noticed it, Józio and his friend entered when Edgar was playing the first few bars and sat in the available seats. (...) When, on the gentle final chord of I B flat major, played with sweetness from the sharp fingers of Edgar, the soft voice of Eliżbeta ceased, there was silence. No one dared to utter a word. One heard the tingling, outside, it was the bell of the last tram to Odesa. The singer took the initiative to put an end to the silence by a reproach to his brother on his use of the pedal. Only then the spell broke. Mrs. Szyller ran to kiss the cheek of her daughter, without making a compliment, invited her to go to bed. - You must be so tired...[4]

---

3 *Ibid.,* p. 121.
4 Iwaszkiewicz 1968, vol. I, pp. 18-19.

This quote should be seen as a realistic and essentially autobiographical description (as much of the book) of what was happening in the lives of young Jarosław and his artist friends in Ukraine, before the Great War changed the course of history and of their existences.

Iwaszkiewicz was oriented by Szymanowski towards refined literary experiments, rich of exoticisms, symbolisms and attractions to Nietzsche's Dionysian. In 1915, encouraged by the composer, Jarosław wrote his first novel, *Ucieczka do Bagdadu* (*Escape to Baghdad*), which aroused the enthusiasm of Szymanowski, who wanted to draw from it an opera libretto. In *Glory and Vainglory*, Edgar (i.e. Karol Szymanowski) and Kazimierz Spychała (who is, in part, an *alter ego* of Iwaszkiewicz himself) talked about "people that exercise power over others" on the beach in Odesa:

- For now, Józio is still completely submissive to your charm, added Edgar. Sometimes we laugh, my mother and I, in hearing him unconsciously imitate your way of speaking, even your Galicianisms... (...) Edgar stood slightly leaning on one elbow and looked at the big, smooth and green waves. He seemed to be talking to himself. - It is certainly a great pleasure to dominate a human being and to ascertain the extent to which he depends on us. They are the first pleasures of power. Beauty is what you see in it... He thinks what you think, feels what you feel... It must be painful to lose such power. The heat had stunned Kazimierz, but he stood up with willpower and took off his jacket and shirt. Undressed, Kazimierz asked in a frowning tone: - When you say this, do you intend to speak about me and Józio? Torn from their thoughts, Edgar thought for a second before answering. - About you? Józio? No, I was talking in general. (...) - I thought most of all, Edgar said while he followed his ideas, I was thinking of people that exercise power over others. How do you acquire this power? In what way do you impose your own personality to another? It is something that I struggle to understand[5].

The theme of the influence on the mind of a young man of some experiences that guided his sensitivity was at the centre of the *incipit* of *Glory and Vainglory* and always remained alive in Iwaszkiewicz.

3. The fall of Tsarism brought with it a plebeian and peasant revolution in Ukraine, which in 1917 shocked the world of Polish estates, with soldiers and peasants attacking many aristocratic houses and killing or forcing to flee the owners; this *jacquerie* generated in Iwaszkiewicz a great aesthetic regret:

---

5 *Ibid.*, pp. 13-14.

In the autumn of 1917 the destruction of the centres of Polish culture in Ukraine began. The news poured in from all sides: the Tymoszówka property, belonging to the Szymanowski; Ryżawka, that of Iwański; Hajworon, that of Rzewuski, fell into the hands of the destroyers. The piano of Szymanowski was thrown into the bottom of a pond, the portrait of Balzac, at Rzewuski, burned; and the collection of paintings of Iwański seized in the small Museum of Human; our aunt Masia's house was demolished, and there were fallen trees in the park and all the area on which the Czernysze residence rose was reduced to a plowed field[6].

While not nationalist, Iwaszkiewicz then enlisted in the III Polish Corps in Ukraine, one of the military formations created in December 1917 by the Poles in the former Tsarist Empire, that consisted of two or three thousand men; they participated in the defense of Kyïv during the first Bolshevik offensive against the independent Ukrainian Republic who in the meantime was proclaimed by the Ukrainian patriots, with even the temporary support of the Poles. The III Polish Corps tried to protect the estates of the Poles in the vast Ukrainian countryside, then clashes with Ukrainian anarchist bands and was eventually disarmed by the Austrians in June 1918. In his first novel, *Hilary, syn buchaltera* [*Hilary, the son of an accountant*], Iwaszkiewicz spoke of his participation in the activities of the III Polish Corps:

I had already told my memories of the past spring with the Third Army Corps, our march from Niemirowo to Uładowki, our skirmishes in that warm early March, with a strong wind from the south. I had talked about all that unspeakable beauty, by which I was fascinated forever, I had recorded with tenderness, in my diary, that military campaign, decorated with violets, poetic stanzas, loyal friends and strong dialogues. Of my stories, he had kept a picture made of sun, heat, leafless oaks along roadsides and rhythmic strokes of cannon[7].

The experience in the III Polish Corps was resumed with more autobiographical and historical details (with a description of its tragic aspects) in *Glory and Vainglory*: Józio - the young character of the novel's first part, who represent one of the Iwaszkiewicz's noble students - enlisted, telling his mother "when you used to read Sienkiewicz to me, it seemed unthinkable that the past that he described would come back one day, absolutely unthinkable! But now, they want to form a Polish cavalry in Vinnycja, as in Sienkiewicz"[8]. Henryk Sienkie-

---

6 Iwaszkiewicz 2010, pp. 150-151.
7 Iwaszkiewicz 1925, pp. 137-138.
8 Iwaszkiewicz 1968, vol. I, p. 123.

wicz was the famous Polish writer, born in 1846 and who received the Nobel Prize in 1905, that wrote the *Trilogy*, namely three historical novels very famous in Poland and set in the Polish-Lithuanian Commonwealth before it was dismembered, therefore before that Poland lost its independence (regained in 1918). *Glory and Vainglory* also described a clash between the Poles and a band of Ukrainians, the disarmament of the Corps by the Austrians, the contacts in Kyïv with one of the organizers of the POW - Polska organizacja Wojskowa [Polish Military Organization], i.e. the painter Henryk Józewski (in the novel he was given the name of Henryk Antoniewski), who would become the Polish governor of the part of Volhynia that was in 1921 assigned to Poland with the Treaty of Riga[9]; then the recruitment into a new Polish Corps under General Haller and the clash at Kaniv on May 1918 with the Germans, who had occupied Ukraine after the surrender of Russia and had ordered the dissolution of the Polish Corps.

Consequently, in June of 1918 Jarosław went to Jelysavethrad, where the Szymanowski family stayed after having abandoned Tymoszówka (their property in the countryside); there the composer asked him to write the libretto of an opera (*King Roger*) set in Sicily: "Staying in the same room, all night we were talking about topics that interested us. At last, he told me of Sicily, of all that he had seen there and what he had read in many books about Italian culture"[10]. After a stay in Kyïv, during which Iwaszkiewicz began to work on the subject of the libretto, the two young men saw each other again in September in Odesa, in Marianna Davidov's villa where the Szymanowski's moved.

Here, on the shores of the Black Sea, our drama was crystallized. [...] The weather was gorgeous, the sky was cloudless and we spent the whole morning on the beach and in the water. In the afternoon we sat on the high bank of the sea and we discussed our works or read my most recent work which I had brought to Odesa[11].

After several changes, *King Roger* was completed in 1924.

4. Following the escape of many young Poles and intellectual friends from Ukraine, Jarosław obtained the documents necessary to

---

9 For a biography of Józewski see Snyder 2005.
10 Iwaszkiewicz 2010, p. 157.
11 Iwaszkiewicz 1983, p. 61.

move to Poland. The fate of Kyïv and Ukraine was uncertain and the city had already tragically changed hands some times since February 1917; that autumn 1918 it was still occupied by the Germans and governed by the Ukrainian general Skoropads'kyj, who had established an autonomous Ukrainian state. The first occupation of the capital by the Bolsheviks, at the end of 1917, had resulted in random executions and the application of the "Red Terror", while in the countryside there were the cited violent peasant's *jacqueries*. The approach of the German defeat announced even more fearsome times, in which Ukraine would become for another three years a battleground between the Bolsheviks, the Tsarist White Army, the bands of peasants, the anarchists, the Ukrainian independentists led by Petljura and the Polish Army.

On 14 October 1918, Jarosław arrived in Warsaw. The escape from the tragedy gave way to an existential drama that fed on an identitarian uneasiness, but never tarnished the refined sensibility and the European horizons that characterized the cultural personality of Iwaszkiewicz. Warsaw was destined to be, as Iwaszkiewicz knew, the place of his future life: "Why have I not already learned oh, my City, to hug you with all the strength of my heart, to give you everything that my lungs contain so I do not alienate now, sobbing and getting lost in your narrow and chaotic streets?"[12]. However, Iwaszkiewicz had quickly found his full standing in the establishment of the new Polish nation: he was one of the protagonists of the new school of poetry, that of "Skamander", which had successfully shaken the Polish literary life.

Fascination for the young Jarosław was evidenced by the words of the then eighteen year old Irena Krzywicka (the writer who became famous for her feminist battles), who attended the first performance of the Skamander poets in the Pikador Café of Warsaw, on 29 November 1918: "Iwaszkiewicz was huge, slender, of rare beauty, with his dreamy eyes and his fleshy and sensual slanted mouth, his indolent grace"[13]. About thirty years later, this atmosphere was evoked, with a mixture of satire and nostalgia, by the caption of a cartoon which appeared in 1947 in the literary magazine *Odrodzenie*: "Perverse Iwaszkiewicz, passionate Wierzynski, unkempt, daydream-

---

12 Iwaszkiewicz 1925, p. 75.
13 Jedlicka, Toporowski 1963, p. 173.

ing Lechon, elegant Tuwin with his birthmark, oh, how the figures of these rising stars of our literature impressed ladies young and old"[14]. In 1922 Jarosław married Anna Lilpop, the daughter of a well-known and wealthy industrialist. Anna was aware of Iwaszkiewicz's bisexuality. In 1923 Iwaszkiewicz was employed as secretary of the President of the Sejm (the Polish Parliament), and had diplomatic tasks in Copenhagen and Brussels. Despite this, Ukraine was always on his mind.

5. Iwaszkiewicz saw Ukraine through the eyes of a Pole, as his "small country" rich in humanity, natural beauty and history, but failed to give it a complete national and cultural identity. According to Ukrainian critics, in *Glory and Vainglory* "The writer shows the disappearance of the world of Polish Kresy and Polish nobility in Ukraine in a way that looks more like a natural disaster, but not as the result of a disastrous history"[15]. But this was only partly true: the two figures of landowners of Podolia that appear in *Glory and Vainglory*, the elderly Royski and Myszyński, were presented as an expression of a social class in decline, aged and inept. Royski was constantly struggling with his delusions of improbable and bankruptcy agronomic innovations, while the old Myszyński lived without affection for his son Janusz and devoted his time, while the world was being engulfed by war and revolution, only to cutting out notes for his old player piano. Moreover, as we saw, in his memoirs Iwaszkiewicz himself was quite frank about social relations among Ukrainian Poles and about the anachronistic closure in itself of the high aristocracy.

Remembering Ukraine in his new life in Warsaw, Jarosław had for Kyïv a sense of distance and inaccessibility:

Kijów, city of pain, a city devastated by the Tartars, ravaged by its own children, a city in great pain. The twilights and the bells of its golden domes were my most precious memories. Purple lavender gardens, blue lines of water and sand, the silver domes of St. Andrew's, bluish woods, for me you all have the same colors and the same moist scent. Often, when I return in the evening, tired of this city (...), I see the red palaces, terraces, the roads clinging to the hills, (...) the trees in the bright April, the blue-domed monasteries, the escarpments of the convents' parks, all covered with broom of gold, and over the grey waters, the wooden palisades, the boys on the road, white summer clouds, and I feel the piercing whistles of the night trains (...). City infinitely sweet, city of my youth, I prefer to see you like in a dream,

---

14 Shore 2006, p. 276.
15 Suchomlynov 2006, pp. 173-174.

in Warsaw... If I really were to see you today, you would appear to me completely different. It was better that I left you, for me you will always be the fairy story of
water, green bushes and night moss[16].

Volhynia was the cradle, the hidden chest, of the ancient Polish
world to the destruction of which Iwaszkiewicz was a witness; as a boy
he had total contact with that region, physical and spiritual, as the
story of a holiday on the estate of Smolivka, owned by Jurij Mikłu-
cho-Makłaj, a friend from Kyïv (also the son of an insurgent of 1863):

Smolivka was an estate in a forest and there wasn't the usual mansion (...). Nearby there was a small village of Polish Catholic *szlachta* [petty nobility]. This unique
corner of the world was a miraculous oasis in the forest, which had guarded the language and customs of the old world, as in the stories of Orzeszkowa. (...) The sur-
roundings of Smolivky were very beautiful. We swam in ponds and rivers, in the
evening we walked with girls or went for mushrooms (...). And how can we forget
the overnight stay at the Jewish inn, which is located on the road between Kijów
and Żytomierz, our journey to the capital of Volhynia, the walks along the Teteriv
shore on the paths on which Kraszewski and Apollo Korzeniowski [i.e. the father of
Joseph Conrad] had walked?[17]

In 1925 Iwaszkiewicz published *Księżyc wschodzi* [*The moon rises*]
which is, he himself admitted in his memoirs, his "beloved" work, a
short novel that has been already defined existentialist and that is set
in Volhynia[18]. The literary reconstruction of that world and its environments fed itself on the descriptions of mansions, of rural labor
(very thorough and full of emotions) and with continued references to the majesty of the natural environment and Ukrainian steppe:

The carriage went slowly, as if walking, on an incredibly wide road, continuing
straight and crossing the streets of the town. The houses, the red glasses for the sun,
hiding behind the gardens. Later, the light pink bricked mill, wrapped in a fog made
of flour and dusk, while the Ros river roared with its stones under the water, then a
couple of houses and a stop, wider road, and everywhere the smell of ripe corn. Antoni sat next to his aunt, quiet - rather, thoughtful, reverent. Yet he hadn't cut ties
with reality. Looked: on the left there was a smooth beet field; along the neat rows
in a soft rosy light, ran the strips of their green leaves; behind the beets one could
see the white sea of the rye and a clear eastern horizon. Nearer, on the road, ran the
elongated shadow of the carriage, which grew longer and longer, finally jumping

---

16 Iwaszkiewicz 1925, pp. 154-155.
17 Iwaszkiewicz 2010, pp. 76-77.
18 On *The Moon Rises* and the Volhynia, see Suchomlynov 2007.

the ditch, full of tall grass and dusty, and running away trembling on the field. On
the right, behind his aunt's black hat, the same endless plain, but reddened by the
fire of the western sunset; each stem of dark wheat was glowing because of the red
glow and was shining. Although it was evening, the night wind was still weak and
every ear stood motionless on the field and still there wasn't the smell of steppe that
Antoni knew well. When he closed his eyes, the smell completely gripped him and
created for him the illusion of inexistent memories. It seemed to him that he was
not raised in the city, not in a narrow street, but, in fact, in a villa like those where
his father walked in summer clothes, of white linen. And where, once out of the
garden, impregnated with the smell of tobacco and wild violets, every night, every
blue night, he breathed that air of the steppe and that smell of ripe rye[19].

Even the flavors came back to bite the memory of the writer exiled
from his native land; the young protagonist of *The moon rises*, which
had the "strange" habit of not drinking, was forced to taste for the
first time *horilka* (i.e. the Ukrainian vodka), along with good ravio-
li or Ukrainian *varenyky*: "with cheese, prepared as usual in Ukraine,
large and tasty as if they hadn't been cooked in a clay oven, but roast-
ed with the summer sun of the harvest"[20].

6. History had torn this idyll. Antoni, the novel's protagonist, was
aware of his Polishness as well as the inevitable decline of the Polish world of Ukraine: "So what? - Antoni thought - What else have
we got to lose? Everywhere is full of our trail and wherever they sink
like a stone in a swamp"[21]. The tone of these inner thoughts of An-
toni-Jarosław was very bitter, but realistic. Iwaszkiewicz was a real-
ist throughout his life, for example by recognizing in 1945 the Polish
communist regime and accepting to carry out a public role as President of the Association of Writers and then as a Member of the Parliament. Some of his Skamander friends, who had instead chosen the
path of exile after the creation of a Stalinist regime in Poland, fierce-
ly criticized his attitude; however, his humanity and his tact avoided
that they would finally break up with him for good or would attack
him publicly. In his own way, Aleksander Wat (a leftist writer, but
anti-Stalinist) protected Iwaszkiewicz in a private conversation made
abroad in 1956 with Mieczysław Grydzewski (the former editor of
Skamander) that heavily accused Iwaszkiewicz. Wat said: "Iwaszkie-

---

19 Iwaszkiewicz 1964, p. 72.
20 *Ibid.*, p. 40.
21 *Ibid.*, pp. 73-74.

wicz has always been (…) an elitist poet. And we need to understand that when the government changed, he continued to have good relations with the elite. The new one"[22]. However, Grydzewski did not break up with Iwaszkiewicz and from his London exile always maintained correspondence with him.

To his Ukrainian native village of Kalnyk, Iwaszkiewicz in 1931 dedicated this poem:

I would like to see the spreading waters
and rolling plain and the sky again,
and not think that this whole world
was stolen from me.
I would like to have a long time to be able to wake up in the night
not to write prose or poems,
but to watch the silvery dew
mist between the lawn and in the reeds.
Look at the bottom of the green waters
my face obscured by the years.
Vain torture of dreams of glory!
How it is past - and so little remained[23].

7. These are words that reveal a real concrete nostalgia, also characterized by simplicity. A simplicity, however, that we must add to the aristocracy that characterized Iwaszkiewicz's complex, and sometimes inscrutable, personality. The anachronism and the disorientation of Iwaszkiewicz in his new life in Warsaw, that there never really ended and that he took with him for almost his entire life, was in fact judged by his contemporaries and critics of aristocratic mold and then with a hint of artifice. Wat questioned, even in the last years of his life, how much there was in Iwaszkiewicz duplicity, on the one hand so much in tune with nature and the mystery, and on the other hand capable of being a diplomat, poet laureate, conciliatory man with power[24].

However, the duplicity is only an effect: Bergson said that disorder is the order that we do not perceive. Iwaszkiewicz's duplicity must have appeared to those who were imbued with the Brechtian paradigm of the unilaterally committed writer, a model that was prob-

---

22 Wat 1989, pp. 236-237.
23 Iwaszkiewicz 1931, p. 86.
24 Shore 2006, p. 336.

ably totally unrelated to Iwaszkiewicz, who instead had a Goethian, most decadent and aesthetic, view of art and of the writer, as capable of grasping the root of the vital flow of existence. Iwaszkiewicz was a "metaphysician of sensuality", as said Czesław Miłosz.

*B*IBLIOGRAPHY

J. Iwaszkiewicz, *Hilaire fils de comptable*, Paris 1925 (first Polish edition: 1923).

J. *Iwaszkiewicz, Książka moich wspomnień* [*The Book of my Memories*], Poznań 2010 (first edition: 1957).

J. Iwaszkiewicz, *Księżyc wschodzi* [*The moon rises*], Warsaw 1964 (first edition: 1925).

J. Iwaszkiewicz, *Powrót do Europy* [*Back to Europe*], Warsaw 1931.

J. *Iwaszkiewicz, Sława i Chwałą* [*Glory and Vainglory*], vol. I, Warsaw 1968 (first Polish edition: 1956).

J. Iwaszkiewicz, "Spotkania z Szymanowskim" ["Meetings with Szymanowski"], in *Pisma muzyczne* [*Writings on Music*], Warsaw 1983.

W. Jedlicka, M. Toporowski (eds.), *Wspomnienia o Julianie Tuwimie* [*Memories of Julian Tuwim*], Warsaw 1963.

C. Miłosz (ed.), *Post-War Polish Poetry*, Berkeley, Los Angeles, London 1982.

J. Morris, "The Polish Terror: Spy Mania and Ethnic Cleansing in the Great Terror", *Europe-Asia Studies*, 56, 5, 2004, pp. 751-766.

M. Shore, *Caviar and Ashes. A Warsaw Generation's Life and Death in Marxism, 1918-1968*, New Haven and London 2006.

T. Snyder, *Sketches from a Secret War*, New Haven and London 2005.

O. Suchomlynov, *Pol's'ko-ukraïns'ke kul'turne pohranyččja u prozi Jaroslava Ivaškevyča (Topika i funkcional'nist')* [*The Polish-Ukrainian cultural border in the prose of Jarosław Iwaszkiewicz (Topical and functionality)*], Ph.D. dissertation, University of Berdyansk 2006.

O. Suchomlynov, "Topičnist' povisti Jaroslava Ivaškevyča *Misjač schodyt'*", ["Placeness in the short novel *The moon rises* of J. Iwaszkiewicz"], *Volyn'-Žytomyrščyna. Istoryko-filolohičnyj zbirnyk z rehional'nych problem*, 17, 2007, pp. 61-70.

A. Wat, *Mon siècle. Confession d'un intellectuel européen*, Paris 1989 (French edition).

6. Independence: Literature, Historiography and Memory of the Ukrainian National Republic (1917-1921)

It was conceived as a contribution to the "The First World War and Its Global Legacies: 100 Years On" (4-6 April 2014) organized by the Faculty of Education and Society at the University of Sunderland (UK), whose Proceedings are being published.

1. For many Kyïvian residents, such as Mikhail Bulgakov, who had not paid enough attention to the many signs of revival of the Ukrainian national consciousness, the fall of the autocracy and the beginning of the Ukrainian state-building represented a rude awakening; those before the war, for Bulgakov

were legendary times, times when a young and carefree generation lived in the gardens of the most beautiful cities of our country. (...) But things turned out quite differently. The legendary times were cut short and history began thunderously, abruptly. I can point out the exact moment it appeared – it was 10:00 a.m. on March 2, 1917, when a telegram arrived in Kiev, signed with two mysterious words: "Deputy Bublikov." I swear that not one person in Kiev knew what these mysterious fourteen letters meant, but one thing I do know, history signaled that something was about to begin. It started and then continued for four years[1].

Two days after the announcement made by the famous telegram, March 17, 1917 (Gregorian calendar), the Central'na Rada, that is the Ukrainian Assembly, was created in Kyïv at the instigation of the moderate Association of Ukrainian Progressives (TUP, then called the Ukrainian Party of Federalist Socialists) and of the Social Democratic Party of Ukraine led by Volodymyr Vynnyčenko, a writer, and Symon Petljura, a journalist. Especially in the early weeks, the peasantry and the urban proletariat were not part of the autonomist movement. On

---

1 Bulgakov 1991, pp. 207-208.

the other hand, a Ukrainian national identity had not yet fully blossomed. Ukrainians were not an important part of the imperial élites; the majority lived in the countryside, and only 5% of the Ukrainians lived in the cities; just over 20% of the Kyïv's inhabitants were Ukrainians (6% in Odesa). Altogether, in 1897, Russian speakers accounted for 11,7% of the tsarist Ukraine population. Then there was the problem of the "Russification" of large parts of the urban and educated Ukrainian population.

Generally, Russians and "Russified" citizens were completely insensitive to Ukrainian aspirations, as noted by the Russian-speaking lawyer of Jewish origin, Aleksej Gol'denvejzer: "in the first weeks, we knew nothing and did not want to know anything about Ukrainism and its national aspirations. Any mention of these issues by interested circles was rejected by us with rudeness and lack of tact."[2] The rural world, if it represented the guardian of language and national traditions, had no political sentiments of the modern type, or national, but mainly regional[3] and dominated by the ancestral "hunger for land" (half of Ukrainian peasants living on less than three desiatine)[4].

The Galician writer Vasyl' Stefanyk summed up the time of the genesis of Ukrainian self-awareness with a dialogue between an old peasant father and his son, who enlists to defend the new Ukraine, and later dies:

The last time Andrij came here: he was a scholar, my boy. Father - he says - now let's fight for Ukraine. -What is Ukraine? And he raised a clod of earth with his saber and said: - Here, Ukraine is here - and put his sword on his chest. - Here is her blood; we're going to take back our land from the enemy. Give me a white shirt, give me clean water to wash. Farewell[5].

2. The Rada declared its support for the Provisional Government, and the historian Mychajlo Hruševs'kyj was appointed as its president. For some months the Rada rivalled the Civic Committee (monopolized by the Russians), which was recognized by the Provisional Government. A large national Ukrainian demonstration was held Sunday, April 1, 1917 on the square in front of St. Sophia's Cathe-

---

2 Gol'denvejzer 1922, p. 168.
3 It was the same for Russian peasants; see: Brooks 1985, pp. 214-45
4 Krawchenko 1990, pp. 106-107.
5 Stefanyk 1940, pp. 37-38.

dral in Kyïv. On April 19, a pan-Ukrainian congress was summoned to Kyïv, which was attended by about 900 delegates from all provinces. The conference gave the investiture of a national parliament to the Rada, to whose presidency Hruševs'kyj was confirmed almost unanimously, as Gol'denvejzer, who was a member of the Civic Committee, remembers:

The hall was packed with young people who had moods and used words that were foreign to me, while white-headed Professor Hruševs'kyj stood at the head of the chairman's table. I remember his magical power over all this rude public. It was enough for him to raise his hand clutching one of white carnations which decorated the table, and the room fell silent[6].

Vynnyčenko and Jefremov (an important literary critic adhering to TUP) were appointed Rada's Vice Presidents; the Mala Rada or a restricted parliamentary committee was also created with about thirty members. In late May, a delegation led by Vynnyčenko went to Petrograd in order to obtain recognition of the autonomy of Ukraine; the delegation received a cold reception from both the Provisional Government and the Soviet of the city. The weakness of the Provisional Government and its military failures favored the Rada's aspirations.

In the first half of June, a military-Ukrainian congress, which was intended to represent the nearly two million Ukrainian soldiers who had been mobilized, appointed their representatives to the Rada, to which were added the deputies appointed by a pan-Ukrainian peasant congress, which met from 1 to 16th June. But in the following months a regular Ukrainian army was not created, because it was strongly opposed by the Russian Provisional Government and because the leaders of the Rada were afraid of not being able to control a regular armed force;[7] this later proved to be one of the main weaknesses of the Ukrainian revolution. On the other hand, the disintegration of the tsarist army had made it almost impossible to effect a mass recruitment among the millions of peasant-soldiers who were no longer prepared to accept a normal commanding hierarchy; the formation of small military units was preferred, made up of volunteers.

---

6 Gol'denvejzer 1922, p. 168.
7 Palij 1976, p. 21.

3. The autonomy of Ukraine was proclaimed in an edict by Rada on June 23, edited by Vynnyčenko, published in Ukrainian, Russian, Polish and Yiddish, and which was given the name of Universal, the same name given to the edicts of the Cossack Hetmanate; this First Universal was proclaimed in a public demonstration in front of Saint Sophia's Cathedral. The symbolist poet Pavlo Tyčyna celebrated the event in the poem *Zolotyj homin* [*Golden Chime*]:

Somewhere in the sky rivers flow/ The mighty rivers of the Lavra and Sofia's bells!... / (...) It was like a priest drunken with prayers / Our Kyïv, -/ That prayed for the whole of Ukraine. / Wonderful Kyïv. / (...) Thousands of eyes... / Suddenly a silence: someone speaks. / Glory! - From thousands of breasts[8].

A few days later, Vynnyčenko was appointed to head a government with a Social Democratic majority, called the General Secretariat. On July 16, an agreement was reached with the Provisional government - announced by a Second Rada Universal - which included recognition of Vynnyčenko's government. On the same day representatives of national parties were aggregated to the Rada. A few days later a solemn session of the Rada was held, in which the representatives of national minorities gave speeches praising the national harmony, each in their own language. A Secretariat for Nationalities was then created, with departments for Jewish, Polish and Russian Affairs. For the Russophiles, "careless contempt for everything that was Ukrainian, was replaced with surprising speed by complete resignation and the awareness of their own impotence"[9].

In late August there was another intervention of the Provisional Government issuing the "Guidelines", which circumscribed powers and areas of the Ukrainian Secretariat. The Bolsheviks continued the centralist and the All-Russian attitudes of the Provisional Government.

4. The presence of the Bolsheviks in Ukraine was not very consistent: in the Russian Constituent Assembly elections in Ukraine they got no more than ten per cent of the vote, which was reduced to about four on the Right Bank; on the other hand, the internal composition of the party suffered from a predominance of Russians who made up more than half

---

8 Tyčyna 1922, pp. 48-50.
9 Gol'denvejzer 1922, p. 181.

of its members, compared to 23% of Ukrainians and about 14 % of militants of Jewish origin.[10] The Bolsheviks participated in the activities of the Rada, but the existence of an autonomous or independent Ukraine was not part of their vision, as one of their leaders, Georgij Pjatakov, a member for a few months of the Mala Rada, said in June of 1917:

Russia cannot exists without the Ukrainian sugar industry, the same can be said for coal (the Donbas), grain (the belt of black soil, etc.). These industries are closely linked with the rest of the industries of Russia. Indeed, Ukraine does not constitute a distinct economic region[11].

On November 20 the Third Universal was issued with which the Rada declared the creation of a Ukrainian Republic in a Russian Federation; the principle of "free development of each nationality present in Ukraine" was enunciated and the "personal-national autonomy" of every individual, not a territorial, but a cultural concept, which had been advanced by the austro-marxists Spranger and Bauer. It provided for the election of a national council of ethnic minorities, which was responsible for regulating matters of education, culture, language, and so on. All Jewish parties, for whom a quarter of the seats were reserved in the Mala Rada, voted in favor of the Third Universal, which guaranteed them the desired autonomy: it was time for a stronger understanding between the Jewish world and the Ukrainian revolution[12].

In the following weeks the first Ukrainian banknotes were printed, in four languages: Ukrainian, Russian, Yiddish and Polish. The Rada also proclaimed the popular ownership of land without compensation. This decision provoked a storm of protest on the part of political parties, institutions and communities related to the Russian and Polish nationalities, in particular; it was also hard for the backlash across the Russian-speaking elite of the capital, while the bureaucracy wearily adapted to the new power and the new language. Bulgakov, who was the son of a professor of theology of the Russian Academy of Kyïv, in *The White Guard* mocks the efforts of his character Tal'berg,- forced by opportunism to devote himself to the study (for Bulgakov ridiculous) of the Ukrainian language[13].

---

10 Borys 1980, p. 89, p. 166, p. 169.
11 Cited in Borys 1980, p. 136.
12 Abramson 1999, pp. 60-61.
13 Bulgakov 2003, p. 28.

In the countryside, the announcement of the Universal, with the joint effects of the Imperial army collapse, led to the start of a great *jacquerie*. Alex Ceslas Rzewuski in his memoirs describes what happened in the palatial residence of Countess Maria Branicka, in Bila Cerkva, where he had been a guest in the spring:

Bolshevik agitators of all kinds easily convinced the peasants. One evening, after dinner, a crowd of peasants invaded the castle and the rooms where there were the Countess and her guests. Everything happened quickly and calmly. The farmers did not make much noise, but declared that freedom had finally arrived and that now the castle was theirs. Then they started to take away the furniture that pleased them. Above all, they sought the treasures that they believed were hidden, tearing the wonderful upholstery and (...), the house caught fire early. (...) It is said that then something curious happened: the same peasants who had looted and burned the house, seeing the countess was leaving, came to kiss her hand, crying[14].

On December 17, the Bolsheviks addressed an ultimatum to the Rada, invoking the alleged aid given to the counter-revolutionary forces of General Kaledin active on the Don. In these dramatic junctures Vynnyčenko, during a meeting of representatives of the Ukrainian society and culture to celebrate the New Year of 1918, failed to make a real toast of good wishes and said: "What can I say? The barbarians of the north are at our door and threatening to trample, to cancel all our achievements, to destroy our young state, to wipe out our culture"[15].

5. On January 25, 1918 with the Fourth Universal, under pressure from the Bolshevik attack, the Rada proclaimed the independence of the Ukrainian National Republic; representatives of the Jewish Socialist Bund party and those of the Russian Mensheviks voted against the Fourth Universal. All the other Jewish parties abstained. The Polish socialists voted in favor of the declaration of independence, while the Polish Democratic Centre abstained (the Polish National Democrats were not part of the Rada). Meanwhile, having created a Soviet republic of Ukraine with Charkiv as capital, on January 29 the Bolsheviks instigated a revolt of the Kyïv's Arsenal workers,

---

14 Rzewuski 1976, pp. 130-131.
15 Dorošenko 1930, p. 91.

which was quelled with difficulty; on February 8, the Ukrainian government decided to leave Kyïv, which had been subjected to ten days' severe bombing:

The casualties among the inhabitants were relatively few, but the destruction was terrible. I believe that at least half of the houses of the city, in one way or another, have been hit by the bombs; the fire produced particularly horrific impressions. (...) The inhabitants of Kiev, although they survived more than a dozen revolutions, evacuation, riots, etc., still remember with particular horror the eleven days of bombing. The majority of the population took refuge in the cellar, in the cold and dark. Shops and markets, of course, were closed; so you had to eat your provisions and what you could find[16].

The Bolshevik troops, by admission of their own commander Antonov-Ovseenko, were composed mainly of Russians[17].

Russian ex-Tsarist officers who took refuge in Kyïv were the main victims of the occupants: more than two thousand of them were shot.[18] Even the Orthodox Metropolitan of Kyïv was executed. The Bolsheviks incited Ukrainian forces in Volhynia; but an armistice between the Bolsheviks and the Central Powers had already been in force since 15 December, which also admitted, on January 6, Ukrainian representatives to the peace negotiations in progress at Brest-Litovsk. On February 9 they signed a peace treaty. An important role in the negotiations had been played by Ukrainian representatives of the Austrian parliament and by the Austrian Archduke William of Habsburg, who had embraced the cause of Ukrainians and aspired to become the ruler of a future independent state of Ukraine.[19] The Ukrainian delegation was able to obtain a secret protocol in which Austria undertook to create a Ukrainian independent kingdom in Galicia and Bukovina. In March, the Bolsheviks too signed a peace treaty with the Central Powers and had to recognize the independence of Ukraine.

6. The German presence in Ukraine brought the law and order to the capital. The Rada fielded a series of reforms. They also introduced the national coat of arms of Ukraine, drawn by Vasyl' Kryčevs'kyj and based on the trident which appears in the currencies of Volod-

16 Gol'denvejzer 1922, p. 204.
17 Antonov-Ovseenko 1924, p. 133.
18 Melgounov 1926, p. 43.
19 On William of Habsburg, see: Snyder 2008.

ymyr the Great. The Germans wanted, for their part, to transform Ukraine into a protectorate and exploit its resources for the war effort. Ideologically distant from the socialist forces that drove the Rada and dissatisfied with their agricultural policy, the Germans matured in the following months the intention of encouraging a coup, which took place on April 29, 1918, when the Assembly of the League of landowners (mainly composed of large and medium Russian or Russified landowners) hailed the former tsarist general of a noble Cossack family, Pavlo Skoropads'kyj, as Hetman or supreme authority of a new Ukrainian state. On April 26, Skoropads'kyj had met General Groener, chief of the German General Staff, to agree on the nature of the new regime. The Rada was dissolved, the right to land ownership was restored, strikes were forbidden, the eight-hour working day was abolished, and a presidential system was created, which was in fact semi-dictatorial. Interestingly, from opposite sides, both Vynnyčenko and the pro-Russian Bulgakov issued derogatory judgments against the putsch that gave rise to the Hetmanate. For Vynnyčenko it was a "militaristic farce. (...) The sparrows on the eaves laugh out loud."[20] Bulgakov notes, with a hint of malice, that "by some curious irony of fate and history, his election (...) had taken place in a circus. A fact which will doubtless provide future historians with plenty of laughs"[21].

Although only a minority of the members of government were formed by Ukrainian patriots, the Hetmanate managed to lay the foundations of the Ukrainian state organization in the military, academic and diplomatic fields; the Hetmanate tried to create an administrative network device and 150 Ukrainian high-schools were established (but only 3 in Kyïv); the teaching of Ukrainian was also made compulsory in Russian schools; two Ukrainian universities were created; substantial funds were spent on printing textbooks in Ukrainian; the Ukrainian Academy of Sciences was established, while the Ukrainian State Theatre was created. The ministries for national minorities were, however, dissolved.

7. The peasants' tenacious opposition to the agricultural policy of the Hetmanate was the main cause of its weakness and its downfall,

---

along with the hostility of the various socialist forces, German mistrust towards the strengthening of the Ukrainian army and the attempt on the part of the tsarist Russians to dominate the government. The peasants, placed under pressure by the German occupiers, but most by landowners' revanchisme, formed armed bands in reaction, that took control of entire areas of the country.

In the following months, the political climate worsened. On 30 July General von Eichhorn, the German military governor, was assassinated by a Russian social revolutionary. The crisis erupted after the final defeat of Germany; to ingratiate himself with the Entente Powers, who were in favor of a restored Russian state, the Hetman formed a new government and on November 14 issued an edict declaring a federation between Ukraine and a revived pan-Russian state. Petljura, in turn, issued a Universal in the name of the Directorate, that brought together the forces of the opposition, calling for an uprising for an independent Ukraine. The army that gathered, apart from the elite units, was made up of volunteers and guided by otamans i.e. local peasants' warlords who did not follow central directives and often indulged in anti-Semitic ideas associating the Jews to the Bolsheviks.

On 21 November 1918, Directorate forces besieged Kyïv. Across the country the forces favorable to the Directory numbered a hundred thousand men in arms. Kyïv capitulated on December 14 after the abdication of Skoropads'kyj (who left the city in disguise a few days later, hidden among the German troops). But the Bolsheviks invaded Ukraine again and, with the help of many peasant bands who had previously supported the Directory, on 3 February 1919 recaptured Kyïv. Bulgakov marks the time of the abandonment of the city by the troops of Petljura with chilling words:

The star of Mars suddenly exploded in the frozen firmament above the City, scattered fire and gave a deafening burst. After the star, the black spaces across the Dnieper, the distance leading to Moscow, echoed with a long, low boom. And immediately a second star exploded in the sky, though lower, just above the snow-covered roofs. At that moment the Blue division of gajdamaki marched over the bridge, into the City, through the City and out of it forever. Behind the Blue division, the frost-bitten horses of Kozyr'-Leško cavalry regiment crossed the bridge at a wolfish lope followed by a rumbling, bouncing field kitchen... then everything disappeared like it had never been[22].

---

22 *Ibid.*, pp. 187-188.

There followed months of chaos: political confusion, social frustration, widespread violence, the eclipse of state authority, the accession of many Jewish workers to Bolshevism, the opposition of major Jewish parties (such as the Socialist Bund) to the independence of Ukraine, the centuries-old rivalry made the Jews the goals of popular violence and of local warlords' lust for power. The Directory leaders, Vynnyčenko (whose wife Rozalia was Jewish) and Petljura, officially condemned the violence against the Jews, but failed to curb its spread. All this created the myth of Ukrainian anti-Semitism, and weighed in the West's judgment about the Ukrainian revolution. Massacres of Jews were actually committed by all the forces: peasants' otamans, White generals, Bolsheviks, Polish troops[23]. It is estimated that the Jewish victims of the pogroms of 1919-20 were between 35 and 50 thousand[24].

The French Foreign Minister Pichon expressed his opposition to Ukrainian independence; the French contingent present in Odesa gave no support or recognition to the Ukrainian Government and retired in early April of 1919. The withdrawal of the French was also provoked by the military successes of the otaman Matvij Hryhoriïv's Cossack troops, which drove the French from Cherson and Odesa.

Hryhoriïv fights against all, in defense of his populace and his districts: the French and the Greeks who had landed in southern Ukraine, the first units of the Polish army formed in Podolia and Bukovina, the White Army of Denikin, the Bolshevik's Red Army, his own allies of the Directory, and the other peasant warlord Machno (a temporary ally of the Bolsheviks), who killed him.

To the epic of Hryhoriïv's Cossacks is dedicated *Čotyry šabli* [*The Four Sabers*] of 1930, Jurij Janovs'kyj's best novel; the protagonists are the otaman Šachaj (i.e. Hryhoriïv) and his three colonels.

Šachaj hears the call of the ancient Cossack chiefs,

all virtuous, brave revelers, pirates of the sea, who proudly trod the land of the great nations, all knights of their unfortunate honor, martyrs. (...) Walking around the church and pausing in front of the holy Cossacks painted on the walls, Šachaj swore to himself not to penetrate the mercy in his heart. He swore that he would not believe in anyone, whether prostrate under his saber or sitting at his table[25].

---

23 Abramson 1999, p. 115.
24 Subtelny 2102, p. 363.
25 Janovs'kyj 1983, p. 173.

Šachaj wanted to defend his revolution, that of the Cossack, peasant, plebeian world, who had finally got rid of the tsarist autocracy and no longer wanted to be submissive to masters: "I swear on my honest lineage, on my servant grandfather, on my great-grandfather, a Cossack: honor and courage are not yet dead. Love and hate, friendship and sacrifice will be resurrected from oblivion. We will not let the revolution perish"[26].

8. During the second Bolshevik occupation of Kyïv, Hetmanate ministers, Ukrainian and Russian nationalists (about seventy members of the Russian nationalistic club) were killed. The intentions that inspired the political police or the Ukrainian Čeka (Vučk) were well illustrated by the "verses" published in February of 1919 in a local Bolshevik bulletin by Vsevolod Balyc'kyj (who became leader in the '20s): "Rivers of blood flow./ So what? May they run. / There will be no forgiveness / Nothing will save you, nothing"[27]. Among the victims of the new Bolshevik occupation, executed on July 8, was the philologist Volodymyr Naumenko, Minister of Education under the Hetmanate. In the Archives of the current Ukrainian security services there is a report, written in red pen, of the skimpy interrogation carried out on him by an officer of Vučk, based on a form. After the responses given by Naumenko there is a death sentence by shooting, to be carried out within 24 hours. The Čeka commissioner's name is absent from the record, and his signature is illegible[28].

One may fill the psychological void of this report with the terrible novelette *Ja (Romantyka)* [*I (Romance)*] by Mykola Chvyl'ovyj, a writer and leading exponent of the national-communism of the Twenties, who committed suicide in 1933 because of the fierce Stalinist repression. The protagonist of the story is a Čekist commissioner who presides over a troika responsible for implementing the Leninist "red terror" in a Ukrainian city. "I spend day and night in the Čeka. Our home is a fantastic palace: it belongs to a nobleman who had been shot. Chimerical doors, antique embroidery, portraits of the royal family. Everything is looking at me from all corners of the room

---

26 *Ibid.*
27 Shapoval 2003, p. 373.
28 Archiv Služby Bezpeky Ukraïny (Archive of Security Services of Ukraine), 68428, 32.

where for the occasion I put my office"[29]. The ruthless Dr. Tagabat and the weak Andrjuša also belong to the troika (the "new Sanhedrin, black court of the City"):

Andrjuša, my poor Andrjuša, was sent here to the Čeka by this impossible Revolutionary Committee, against his weak will! And Andrjuša, this dour Communist, always hesitates when he has to put his energetic signature to a death sentence "shoot"; he always signs like this: he writes on the severe act of death not his name or last name, but a Hittite hieroglyphic, which is absolutely incomprehensible, chimerical[30].

The story describes the progressive degradation of the protagonist, whose romantic revolutionary fervor is frozen in a mechanical reflection and bestial murder, which led him finally to personally execute the death sentence of his mother, captured while she was praying in a convent with nuns.

9. In the countryside, the Bolsheviks alienated the sympathies of the peasants by trying to bring them together in communes and sending from Russia thousands of agents to deal with the seizure of crops; this was followed by numerous peasant uprisings which lasted for several years. But on August 31, 1918, the capital was to have a new master: Ukrainian troops and the white army of Denikin conquered the city; the Kyïvians welcomed as liberators the new occupants, while family members of missing persons had to identify the bodies of executed prisoners, abandoned by the Bolsheviks. This time the release was dark and fearful; the Whites carried out robberies and acts of anti-Jewish violence; the Bolsheviks and their allies were put to the sword.

In December, the Bolsheviks came back for the third time and famine was the greatest effect of their presence: there were severe shortages of water, heating and food, resulting in a serious epidemic of typhus. In April 1920 Petljura, who for several months was the only voice of the Ukrainian government, signed, as the ultimate and supreme resource of war, an alliance with Piłsudski, the president of Poland. Petljura had to accept Polish sovereignty in Galicia and in the city of L'viv, won in the previous months by the Polish army in

---

29 Chvyl'ovyj 1980, p. 34.
30 *Ibid.*, p. 36.

a fierce war against the Western Ukrainian Republic, which had cost thousands of deaths. Even the return of land ownership to the Polish minority was part of the protocol signed by Petljura and the Polish state. Piłsudski, although an ally of Denikin, did not move to prevent Denikin's defeat by the Bolsheviks because he wanted to impose a border more favorable to Poland. The Ukrainian-Polish forces regained Kyïv in May. The Polish writer Jarosław Iwaszkiewicz, born in Ukraine, describes in his novel of 1923 *Hilary, syn buchaltera*, how on those days the Poles bestowed triumphal honors on Piłsudski:

The flags flutter in the wind, the rifles crackle, cannons thunder, cars screech on the paved streets: Who is he who flew on the steppes, the fields, the dusty roads (...)? That is Joseph Piłsudski marching on Kijów (...) From our balcony we watched the crowd, which escorted him triumphantly, under a harvest, a shower of flowers, with a cheer that could be heard everywhere, coming from every direction, like a rose in spring, a unanimous cry[31].

The Soviet reaction was swift and also used nationalistic motives, calling for all Russians without distinction of class; many former Tsarist officers, including several White prisoners, enlisted in the Red Army, while the same commander-in-chief of the army under the Provisional Government, General Brusilov, launched a manifesto in the columns of *Pravda* in defense of "our beloved Russia." This was followed by the counter-offensive of the Red Army, who recaptured Kyïv after five weeks.

"We went out for a while, we went back forever", boasted an inscription on the walls of the University of Kyïv. In October, Russians and Poles signed an armistice and the last attempt on the part of Petljura to attack the Bolsheviks failed in November of 1921. All Ukrainian prisoners were put to the sword and the survivors, having crossed the Polish border, were interned by the Warsaw government. Petljura continued to lead the Ukrainian government in exile in Paris and became a promoter of a Promethean League, of governments in exile and representatives of the peoples oppressed by the Soviet state; this League had some success and opened branches in many capitals of Europe and Asia. The risk represented by Petljura grew in the eyes of the Soviets with the coup on 14 May 1926 in Poland that led to the dictatorship of Piłsudski: the specter of a new Ukrainian-Polish

---

31 Iwaszkiewicz 1925, p. 156.

alliance was dissolved two weeks later with the assassination of Petljura. The operation was ordered by the GPU and conducted in Paris by the agent Michail Volodin, who instigated the perpetrator of the murder[32].

Michajl Semenko, the founder of Ukrainian Futurism, wrote this poem against Petljura during the Polish-Bolshevik war: "He pressed the button with his finger / the Entente. / They responded in the morning. / Ready - Warsaw? / Shake Petljura - / it is the hour - / May the bands be brought out - / against the communes. / - *Pan* [Master] ordered. / And work has started. Brother against brother. / Deceived - against workers / in an enemy attack. On the front, betrayal - / and they took the red Kyïv... / Is it not clear to all? / Are there not enough red fires? / The revolution is still burning perfectly, / smiling at tomorrow". Semenko was part of the young left-wing intellectuals who supported the creation of the Bolshevik regime, but then become progressively conscious of its true face and ended up shot in Kyïv in 1937; in this composition he expressed some Bolshevik ideas on Petljura and Poland, which with Stalin were amplified and made fixed ideas.

---

32 Palij 1995, pp. 189-190.

H. Abramson, *A Prayer for the Government: Ukrainians and Jews in Revolutionary Times, 1917-1920*, Cambridge (Mass.) 1999.

V.A. Antonov-Ovseenko, *Zapiski o graždanskoi vojne* [*Notes on the Civil War*], vol. I, Moscow 1924.

J. Borys, *The Sovietization of Ukraine. 1917-1923*, Edmonton 1980.

J. Brooks, *When Russia Learned to Read. Literacy and Popular Literature, 1861-1917*, Princeton 1985

M. Bulgakov, *Notes on the Cuff and Other Stories*, Ann Arbor 1991.

M. Bulgakov, *Belaja Gvardija* [*The White Guard*], Moscow 2003.

M. Chvyl'ovyj, *Ja (Romantyka)* [I (Romanticism)], in *Tvory. V P''ja toch tomach Tvory* [*Works, in Five Volumes*], Vol. II, New York, Baltimora, Toronto 1980.

D. Dorošenko, *Vojna i revoljucija na Ukraine* [*War and revolution in Ukraine*], in S. Alekseev, N. Popov (eds.), *Revolucija na Ukraine po memuaram belych* [*Revolution in Ukraine in White's memories*], Moscow and Leningrad 1930.

A. Gol'denvejzer, *Iz kievskich wospominanij (1917-1921)* [*Memories of Kiev (1917-1921)*], in I.V. Gessen, *Archiv russkoj revoljucii* [*Archive of the Russian Revolution*], vol. VI, Berlin 1922.

J. Iwaszkiewicz, *Hilaire fils de comptable*, Paris 1925 (first Polish edition: 1923).

J. Janovs'kyj, *Čotyry šabli* [*The Four Sabers*], in *Tvory* [*Works*], vol. II, Kyïv 1983 (first edition: 1930).

B. Krawchenko, "The Social Structure of the Ukraine in 1917", *Harvard Ukrainian Studies*, XIV, 1-2, 1990, pp. 97-112.

S.P. Melgounov, *The Red Terror in Russia*, Westport (CT) 1926.

M. Palij, *The Anarchism of Nestor Machno, 1918-1921. An Aspect of the Ukrainian Revolution*, Washington 1976.

M.Palij, *The Ukrainian-Polish Defensive Alliance, 1919-1921*, Toronto 1995.

A. C. Rzewuski o.p., *Á Travers l'invisible cristal. Confessions d'un dominican*, Paris 1976.

I. I. Shapoval, "Vsevolod Balickij, bourreau et victime", *Cahiers du monde russe*, 2003, n. 2-3, pp. 369-401.

T. Snyder, *The Red Prince. The Secret Lives of a Habsburg Archduke*, New York 2008.

V. Stefanyk, *Syny* [*Sons*], in *Vona – zemlja ta inši novely* [*She – The Earth, and Other Stories*], Cracow 1940.

O. Subtelny, *Ukraine. A History*, Toronto 2102 (fourth edition).

P. Tyčyna, *Zolotyj homin. Poeziï. (Zbirka zbirok)* [*Golden Chime. Poems. (Collection of Collections)*], L'viv-Kyïv 1922.

V. Vynnyčenko, *Vidrodžennja naciï* [*The Rebirth of the Nation*], Kyïv and Vienna 1920.

7. *Between Literature and Cinema:* Shadows of Forgotten Ancestors

Paper presented at the conference "Camera-Stylo: Intersections in Literature and Cinema" which was held at the University of Sydney (Australia), School of Letters, Art and Media, from 8 to April 10, 2015.

1. Tall, slender, bald, with a well-trimmed moustache and goatee, and a gaze at times sad, at others too confident[1], always impeccable in his formal dress, Mychajlo Kocjubyns'kyj appeared to the poet Mykola Černjavs'kyj who met him in Chernihiv in 1901, as "an elegant middle-aged gentleman, with a genial face, who looked like a white crow in a flock of black crows"[2]. Kocjubyns'kyj was born on September 17, 1864 in Vinnycja, the city on the Eastern Buh river and current capital of Podolia; this fertile region of Ukraine, which is a couple of hundred kilometers southwest of Kyïv and is separated, on the south, by the Dnister from Moldova, had been annexed to the Russian Empire after the partition of Poland at the end of the eighteenth century. Kocjubyns'kyj lived in Podolia until 1898, when he moved to Chernihiv in northern Ukraine, where he found a job thanks to Borys Hrinčenko (writer and Ukrainian's publishing pioneer), as director of Statistical Office of the local *zemstvo*, the administrative body that had been set up in the framework of the reforms of Alexander II.

The contradiction inherent in the very nature of the writer and artist weighed on his inner life: as the **first-person narrator** of *Intermezzo* (one of his later works) says: "I cannot be alone. I must confess that I envy the planets, which have their orbits and nothing can hin-

---

1 Potupejko 1962, p. 164.
2 Cited in Siundiukov 2002.

der their path. But I encounter on my way, always and everywhere, Man"[3]. - an uneasiness that was exacerbated by the anxiety of perfection of content and style typical of the Ukrainian writer; as he says in a letter to his mistress, Aleksandra Aplaksina: "it is very bad to be a writer. You feel constantly that you have a duty, your eyes are constantly inquiring and wide open (...). It is still not enough. (...) You feel that you're suffering as a poor, inadequate tool, unable to fulfill your task"[4]. In a letter of 1905 he thus described the psychological parable of his creativity:

When I elaborate a plot, in my imagination as long as I portray people, actions and environments, I feel happy: everything seems so bright, so fresh, so full and strong that I tremble with excitement. But all I have to do is sit at my desk and take pen in my hand, and everything that comes from the pen is so pale, anemic and colorless; words fail me when I try to return to what a moment before I had felt so strongly. When I have finished the work, I feel disgust - how miserable it seems to me! If I could limit the creative process to the imagination alone, I would be very happy. But something strong draws me to literary work, and I have devoted all of myself to literature[5].

When, in 1911, he had to re-read some of his early works which Gor'kij wished to have translated into Russian, he confessed: "how much schmaltz and idealization of the peasantry, that primitive technique and what infinite boredom! I blush at re-reading it"[6]. Even the writing of *Shadows of forgotten ancestors* (*Tini zabutych predkiv*) did not satisfy him and he wished to write a longer and more in-depth work on the life of the Hucul people.

This intimate dissatisfaction and anxiety for perfection eventually curbed Kocjubyns'kyj's creativity; he actually did not write much, and never had the opportunity or the courage to grapple with the drafting of a great novel. The story and the short novel were the genres that he actually preferred. The reasons for this choice, however, are eminently stylistic. For Kocjubyns'kyj the word was all; for him, writing was a kind of total art that bordered on painting and music. Indeed, he was pursuing a literary style that was really a form of "writ-

---

3 Kocjubyns'kyj 1974a, p. 297.
4 Letter to Aleksandra Aplaksina (16.7.1910), in Kocjubyns'kyj 1975b, p. 61.
5 Letter to Mychajlo Močul's'kyj (17.11.1905) in Kocjubyns'kyj 1975a, p. 43.
6 Letter to Mychajlo Mohyljans'kyj (26.1.1911), in M. Kocjubyns'kyj 1975a, p. 103. Mohyljans'kyj was one of the transaltors of the Kocjubyns'kyj's works in Russian.

ten" pictorial art. He wanted the word to be similar to a brush-stroke and it had to have the same expressive power as the colors of a painting, replacing the vision to give the psychological sense of the circumstances narrated. Music, then, has a role both in the plots and in the architecture of his writing. It is through a musicality so original as to be demonic that Ivan Palijčuk, the protagonist of *Shadows of forgotten ancestors*, expresses his tragic individuality; and it is always music, that of his simple and delicate ditties, which allows his beloved Marička to appease the anxiety and loneliness of the protagonist.

2. Critics are still debating how to classify the literary work of Mychajlo Kocjubyns'kyj. Surely this is an author of European stature, both for the quality of his writing, the personal psychology, and the links and references to important authors of European literature, and not only the Slav ones. In fact, ever since 1906 his works have been translated into German, Hungarian, Romanian, Swedish, Estonian, Polish, Czech and Russian. In addition, he was a careful reader of continental literature, with a preference for the Scandinavians and German Symbolists.

Kocjubyns'kyj's original reworking of realism reached its full maturity with *Shadows of forgotten ancestors*. The direction taken was definitely that of psychological impressionism, able to penetrate the most intimate folds of the human soul, and to describe nature with tones and accents that give the feeling of being confronted with a filmed and chromatic description of the environments described, with the use of analogical, anthropomorphic and expressive terms. The critical question that remains to be resolved is the following: did Kocjubyns'kyj really approach what is called Modernism in European literature and forms of decadentism? Solomija Pavlyčko denies this strongly, qualifying Kocjubyns'kyj's work in terms of evolved realism, with an impressionistic mold. Indeed, he was a moderate innovator, too aware of the tastes of the Ukrainian public to venture into excessive experimentalism. However it is true what the Romanian (Hungarian speaking) Ukrainist Magdalena Laszlo-Kuciuk says, that the literary vein of Kocjubyns'kyj is an "irrational-introverted type, which filters reality through his sensitivity and for which are important, not the acts themselves, but their reflection in the human soul"[7].

---

7 Laslo-Kucjuk 2000, pp. 200-201.

In his last years Kocjubyns'kyj accentuated his Impressionism and perhaps Oksana Pachlovska is closer to the truth when she defines the work of Kocjubyns'kyj as "a rich laboratory where the between the demands of realism and those of Modernism clash, marking the victory of the latter"[8]. On the other hand, examples of Decadentism's techniques are not lacking in Kocjubyns'kyj's mature prose. Danylo Struk had spoken, for example, of Kocjubyns'kyj's attachment to "neronism", i.e. the tendency to transform the artist's depression into literary material[9]. In the work that we are presenting, Ivan's passiveness in the face of Palahna's betrayal is an example. And then, even more, his half-conscious surrender, almost desired, to the *njavka*, which he knows to be and not be the beloved Marička:

He was caught in two conflicting states of consciousness. He perceived that Marička was close to him and he knew that Maricka was no more of this world, that it was someone else who was taking him towards nothingness, to the wild hills, to lose him. But he felt good, he followed her laughter and happy cries, not fearing anything, light and happy, as before[10].

In this sense, Stefanija Andrusiv called Ivan a typical decadent-secessionist hero[11], whose apparently unmotivated anxieties, whose destructive dreams and mirages form the fabric of an aesthetic of the pathological. The scene that closes the novel is extraordinary and decadent, with an almost active participation of the body of the deceased, in a context in which the incipient decomposition of the corpse becomes a form of communication:

Ivan's yellow face was quietly lying on the sheet, expressing something that only he knew, and the right eye looked jaded, slightly raised from under the eyelid, the pile of copper coins on his chest, and hands folded around a burning candle (...). The body was ready for departure. Whitish spots, such as lichens, spread over him with a barely perceptible shadow. (...) On the face of the dead man, spots had appeared, as if hidden thoughts disturbed him, constantly changing his expression[12].

---

8 Pachlovska, 1998, p. 652.
9 Struk, *Mykhailo Kotsiubyns'kyi: The Modernist Prose Writer*, unpublished manuscript (available on the website of the University of Toronto).
10 M. Kocjubyns'kyj, *Tini zabutych predkiv*, in Kocjubyns'kyj 1974b, p. 217.
11 Andrusiv 2004.
12 M. Kocjubyns'kyj, *Tini zabutych predkiv*, in Kocjubyns'kyj 1974b, pp. 224-226.

With *Shadows of forgotten ancestors*, the meeting between the impressionistic-modernist sensivity of Kocjubyns'kyj and the mythological world view of the Huculs, the Carpathian people who figure in the novel, produced an approach to a genre that can be called magical realism, for the simultaneous co-existence of men, animals and demons and the action - alongside those of nature, the human psyche and the social - of numinous forces and phenomena. It also represented a fusion between the stylistic trends typical of European literature and the ethnography of Ukraine which, together with the whole literary work of Kocjubyns'kyj, produced a more definite inclusion of the Ukrainian literary tradition within the European context.

3. *Shadows of forgotten ancestors* was written - after some years of incubation - in Chernihiv, in a month and a half, from August 20 to October 3, 1911, and was published in early 1912. Kocjubyns'kyj had always had a "ethnographic" vocation and an interest in the exotic. He had worked for five years, from 1892 to 1897, for the commission investigating the damage done by phylloxera to the Crimea and Moldova vines and his inquiring eye had settled on the life of Crimean Tatars and Moldovans, to whom he had dedicated some of his works. The environment of the Galician intellectuals encouraged him to become interested in the Ukrainian Carpathian populations; especially the ethnographer Volodymyr Hnatjuk, Secretary General of the Shevchenko League. Hnatjuk informed him of his research among the Huculs, which gave rise in 1907 to the publication of an extensive collection of *kolomyjky* (songs of the Carpathians) and culminated with the release in 1912 of the two volumes of *Contributions to Ukrainian demonology*[13]; thanks to his acquaintance with Hnatjuk, Kocjubyns'kyj already knew many of the facts reported in the book and he used them for writing the novel. Indeed, the idea of writing a novel about the Huculs had been suggested several times by the same Hnatjuk.

But Kocjubyns'kyj's holidays in the summers of 1910 and 1911 in Kryvorivnja, the Carpathian resort where Hnatjuk, Franko, Stefanyk and many other Galicians intellectuals spent their summer holidays, took on an important role in the genesis of the novel. As Hnatjuk reported in his memoirs, Kocjubyns'kyj, with the help of a local

---

13 Hnatjuk 1912.

teacher, began to collect ethnographic material by talking to people in the region, rambling on the summer sheep pastures, and taking part in festivals and rituals, like the funeral ceremony which closes the novel; Hnatjuk also reported that Kocjubyns'kyj was struck by some of the Hucul social phenomena such as family feuds and adulterous relationships.[14] In a letter dated 1910 to Gor'kij, Kocjubyns'kyj expressed his enthusiasm for the world of this mountain people:

If you only knew how extraordinary, almost fabulous, is this corner of the world, pure and fresh, as if it were born yesterday, with its mountains and lush green, with its eternally roaring mountain rivers. The clothes, the costumes, the whole way of life of the Hucul nomads, who spend all summer with their flocks on the heights of the mountains are so original and picturesque, that you feel transported to a new, unknown world[15].

A year later, during his second stay in the Carpathians, Kocjubyns'kyj wrote to Gor'kij:

I spend all my time hiking in the mountains and riding a hucul horse, light and graceful as a ballerina. I was in wild places, accessible to few, and the pastures. (...) The Huculs are a people with a rich imagination, with a characteristic psyche. Deeply pagan, the Hucul spends his whole life, until his death, in the fight against evil spirits that live in the woods, mountains and waters. He uses Christianity only to beautify his pagan worship. What a great number of fairy tales, legends, folk beliefs and symbols can be found here! I collect the material, live nature, look, listen and learn[16].

This is a taste for the "primitive" that Kocjubyns'kyj shares with the art, culture and psychology of his century; it is a drive similar to that underlying the archeo-psychology of Freud's *Totem and Taboo* and Jung's survey on collective symbolism, which moves Kocjubyns'kyj to know the rites, the wisdom and the way of being in the world by peoples - like the Huculs, but also, in their way, the Capri fisherman - on which the mantle of civilization seems not to have been thrown. Kocjubyns'kyj's interest in the "exotic" (and in the case of the Huculs it is a "nearby" exotic) is an interest for the unconscious

---

14 Kocjubyns'kyj 1914, p. 21.
15 Letter to Maksim Gor'kij (27.8.1910), in Kocjubyns'kyj 1975b, p. 69.
16 Letter to Maksim Gor'kij (16.7.1911), in Kocjubyns'kyj 1975b, p. 126. The notebooks containing the material collected by Kocjubyns'kyj were published in M. Kocjubyns'kyj 1974b, pp. 341-355.

forces that dominate the lives of individuals and communities[17]. In a letter to his wife in 1898, speaking of Ukrainian traditional Christmas Eve customs, he says, "they have a meaning for me, they speak to me of happy childhood memories, and bring with them the poetry of ancient, ancestral times"[18]. In a tale of 1908 Kocjubyns'kyj had already mentioned "the ancestors, living in us, ancestors who for centuries have carried out their sacred rites in the woods"[19].

Ethnography therefore as a highway towards the collective unconscious and the knowledge of those forces, collective and tragic, that govern the fate of individuals, according to a perspective that makes one think, once again, of the bitter analysis of Freud in his latter years, that of *Civilization and Its Discontents*. If there is indeed a constant in the poetic works of Kocjubyns'kyj, it is the failure of the individual and of his secret aspirations, often because of social pressure. Rubchak spoke, in this regard, about an eternal clash in Kocjubyns'kyj between the mythology of the individual, and collective mythology -, that is, between creativity and individual freedom and the suffocating mean established by the founders of the social rituals. A clash that sees the individual always succumbing[20]. In a letter to Čykalenko, the patron and Ukrainian publisher, Kocjubyns'kyj had written: "I have no great hopes in our society. It is still too weak and fragile not to have to ask individuals for anything but sacrifices, while it avoids taking on any obligation or sacrifice for individuals"[21].

In his short essay Feliks Štejnbuk showed how the center of the novel is what he calls the "corporeal existence" of the protagonist[22]. That is to say that in the novel Kocjubyns'kyj follows the existential parable of Ivan, articulated at times when, thanks largely to dance, his body discovers his person, his inner identity. Ivan realizes that, for him, the absence of Marička is unbearable, she who had cured his "strange" energy, who had socialized his diversity (such that, as a child, his mother thought that he was a "changeling", i.e. the son of

---

17 The attraction of Kocjubyns'kyj for psycho-cultural studies can be confirmed by the presence, in his library, of the Russian translation of Lombroso's *The Man of genius*. See: Bestjuk 2006, p. 7.
18 Letter to Vira Deyša (12.1.1896), in Kocjubyns'kyj 1974c, p. 61.
19 M. Kocjubyns'kyj, *Jak my ïsdyly do krynyci*, in Kocjubyns'kyj 1974b, p. 11.
20 Rubchak 1981, pp. 91-92.
21 Cited in Siundiukov 2002.
22 Štejnbuk 2010.

a she-devil, who had been put in place of the real Ivan)[23]. A prerequisite and outcome of the philosophical novel is therefore, according Štejnbuk, that death occurs when finally the individual knows himself. It should, however, be said that it is not a discovery or a therapeutic release, in the way that the parallel Freudian route can be interpreted, but tragic; thus the humanism of Kocjubyns'kyj does not have an optimistic foundation, but seems to adhere to the vitality and the tragic sense of life that was typical of the Huculs.

The reader accustomed to philosophical or theological topics may note with interest in the novel the brief but significant insert, i.e. the dualistic story of the genesis of the universe (perhaps of Bogomilian origin) narrated to Ivan by the *spuzar*, the young servant shepherd and he will perceive the non-random or unaware nature of his presence. Indeed, the novel as a whole seems to join the Gnostic-pagan ontological dualism which proposes the principle of good and evil as co-eternal, although there is also a veneer of Christianity in this dualism, illustrated by the role of the enterprising villain, but originally devoid of legs and arms, played by the devil who stands before God in the primitive myth told by the *spuzar*.

The truth which the primordial numinosity and pagan dualistim of the Huculs opens to Kocjubyns'kyj's surprised, inquiring glaze and to the reader, is the relentless and continuous circle of love and death[24]. Like the agave which appears in the last lines of *The Island* - the story written by Kocjubyns'kyj a few months before his death and dedicated to Capri; "It - the agave - blooms to die and dies to bloom"[25].

4. There have been authors who used Ukrainian demonological figures; examples are the *čorty* (little devils) who populate Gogol's stories, - in Russian but set in Ukraine - or *rusalky* (freshwater sirens), protagonists of a romantic poem by the Polish writer Józef Bohdan Zaleski, mentioned also in the first poem of Ševčenko, the great Ukrainian romantic poet. In the early twentieth century, interest in folk mythology was a literary phenomenon that involved several Ukrainian authors, in the context of the recovery of the popular roots of a language, a culture and a nation rediscovering itself; among

---

23 The legend is described in Hnatjuk 1912, vol. II, p. 199.
24 Some interesting ideas of this kind are included in Salij 2011.
25 M. Kocjubyns'kyj, *Na ostrovi*, in Kocjubyns'kyj 1974b, p. 294

the authors who elaborated texts that could be called neo-mythological, we find Lesja Ukraïnka, Hnat Chotkevyč and Ivan Franko. For a particular sincronicity, by the way, Lesja Ukraïnka wrote his famous drama in three acts *Lisova Pisnja* (*The Song of the Forest*), in which the protagonist is a *mavka* falling in love with a human, in the same summer of 1911 when Kocjubyns'kyj composed *Shadows of Forgotten Ancestors*. Chotkevyč lived in the Carpathian Mountains for a few years and frequented the Hnatjuk's circle; he expressed a negative opinion on the content of *Shadows of Forgotten Ancestors*, because he was more interested in a comprehensive transposition of the Hucul's folk culture, more than in a literary reinterpretation[26]. Lesja Ukraïnka, who also did not like the other works of Kocjubyns'kyj, judged instead *Shadows of Forgotten Ancestors* as an "ecstatic" work[27].

In general, the Ukrainian neo-mythologism or magical realism, as we have seen, is psychological and philosophical; it is an expression of "an effort to understand the deep bonds and laws of the universe, through the prism of myth"[28]. In Kocjubyns'kyj's novel, in particular, transformation and reinterpretation of the myth prevail, which is almost never transposed as such. About Kocjubyns'kyj's mythmaking we can say what Wittegnstein said of Freud, namely, that he did not interpret the myth but, on that basis, created a new one; in place of Freud's rational-psychological hermeneutics, Kocjubyns'kyj produced a literary hermeneutics, a kind of poetry in prose "simple, mystical and deeply tragic"[29].

5. One of the protagonists of *Shadows of forgotten ancestors* is the natural environment of the Carpathians. The author presents it to us from at least three different descriptive angles coming close here, more than anywhere else, to the ideal of making his prose a form of total art: poetic, musical and colored. The first angle, more objective but full of nuances and anthropomorphism ("the black firs incessantly poured their sadness onto Čeremoš, who dragged it away and told of it"),[30] is made of real filmed scenes in which the written word seems to replace the human eye (and camera lens):

---

26 Bestjuk 2006, p. 5
27 Čyževs'kyj 2003, p. 557.
28 Bestjuk 2006, p. 8.
29 Bilec'kyj 2011, p. 308.
30 M. Kocjubyns'kyj, *Tini zabutych predkiv*, in Kocjubyns'kyj 1974b, p. 179.

the distant mountains opened their peaks one after another, arched their backs and fell like waves in the blue ocean. It seemed that the undertow of the waves had stopped just at the moment when the storm raised it from the bottom to throw it over the land and flood the world. The peaks of the Bukovyna already held up the horizon with blue clouds: nearby Synyci, Dzembronja and Bila Kobyla were wrapped in blue, Ihrec' smoked, Hoverlja stung the sky with its pointed spire and Čornohora pressed down on the earth with its heavy body[31].

Some elements of nature, like the torrential river flowing in the valley, the Čeremoš, or the highest mountain range in the background, the Čornohora, are often called by name and described with tones and accents that make them live protagonists of the plot of the novel.

In a second sense, nature seems to accompany and transmit intimate changes in awareness of the human characters of the novel: when the shepherds, after gathering the flock on the heights, invoke divine grace: "The sky was listening tenderly to their sincere prayer; the Beskyd chain frowned benevolently and the wind blew gently, delicately combing the grass of the pasture, like a mother does with her baby's little head..."[32]. Finally, the natural elements often take on a symbolic role in the narrative; for example, when the fence of the sheepfold begins to "whine" relentlessly, always a sign of danger looming over the lives of men and their flocks, personified by the Huculs as *áridnyk* - the devil, the lord of the mountain:

The fence begins a lament similar to that of a trapped fly, whining at the unbearable pain, crying out of solitary sadness... Zz-z... zzi-i... incessantly, relentlessly. It rends the veins and breaks the heart like a knife. You would like not to listen, but you cannot; you would run away, but where? (...). Zz-zz-zyy... Similarly to aching teeth, with their monotonous and unbearable pain. Clench your teeth and be silent. Have pain. Buzz, to hell with you! What use is crying? It's clear that it's "him". May he be turned to stone![33]

6. The best known and most unusual scene of the novel is the final one, where Kocjubyns'kyj describes a funeral ceremony enacted by some Hucul groups, which he had personally witnessed during his stay in the Carpathians. It is an evident rite of exorcism, performed

---

31 *Ibid.*, p. 190.
32 *Ibid.*, p. 192.
33 *Ibid.*, pp. 193-194.

to remove the presence and fear of death with games and erotic rituals. So Kocjubyns'kyj had described the ritual in a letter to Aplaksina:

In one village I came across a original rite. One night an old woman died, and people from *chaty* [traditional Ukrainian houses] converged on her house (here houses are located at a distance of a few *versts* from each other). The dead woman was on the bench next to the wall with burning candles in front of her. Benches were placed in rows in the room, as if it were a theater, and on them sat a lot of people. In the vestibule, next to the dead woman, groups of young people had gathered with the intention of having fun. And what games they played! Their laughter echoed incessantly, jokes, kisses, screams, while the dead woman lay with her pursed, afflicted lips, and the candles burnt down slowly, giving off the typical funeral glow. And so it was for the whole night[34].

This scene of the novel, as well as adding extra originality to the work and sense of surprise to the reader, can be seen in an autobiographical sense, as a kind of foreshadowing of the death of the author, who, already ill, died a year and a half after writing it. The description of Ivan, who watches these games, ends like this: "the corners of his mouth were turned up, as if fixed in bitter reflection: What is our life? A glow in the sky, like the flowers of the cherry tree..."[35] It is as if Kocjubyns'kyj wanted to send a message from the after-life to those who survive, revealing life's transient and cyclic sense and how the dead can also talk to the living.

7. In *Shadows of forgotten ancestors* Kocjubyns'kyj uses Hucul dialect words to indicate all objects of daily use and the local flora (Kocjubyns'kyj and his wife were fond of botany), while also preserving the demonological dialect terminology. In writing this novel, Kocjubyns'kyj sometimes also introduced nouns and verbs derived from dialect, without spoiling the overall intelligibility of the work for the Ukrainian reader and without deviating from the standard linguistic norm. So, in the novel, the reader will meet the *chata* - the traditional Ukrainian habitation; the *kresanja* - the typical Hucul felt hat often decorated with flowers and colorful feathers; the *flojara* - the Carpathian elongated flute; the *trembita* – the Hucul wooden trumpet used to communicate between the valleys, mountains and scattered

---

34 Kocjubyns'kyj 2008, pp. 182-183.
35 M. Kocjubyns'kyj, *Tini zabutych predkiv*, in Kocjubyns'kyj 1974b, p. 226.

houses of Hucul'ščyna (the Ukrainian name of the region), now widely known thanks to the singer Ruslana who introduced it to international pop music; the *keptar* - the sleeveless leather vest; the *bartka,* or Hucul axe; the *postoly* - Hucul sandals, etc. The demonological central entity of the novel is the *njavka* (Ukrainian: *mavka*), a woodland nymph that appears in the form of a beautiful girl, but who has a horrible gash on her back that makes her internal organ visible; she bewitches and drags into the abyss young shepherds and woodcutters. The mortal enemy is the furry, fat and comical *čuhajstyr,* who loves to dance the frenzied Hucul dances. Looming over all creation is "he", the devil (*áridnyk*), which is considered the true creator of the mountains and would like to compete with God; in the form of *ščeznyk* (a demon that appears and disappears suddenly) he may show himself to the shepherds in the mountains.

In short, from these formative elements is derived a work that appears to the reader as original, free of restraints of genre or content, a unique work - *Shadows of forgotten ancestors.*

8. On the centenary of the birth of Kocjubyns'kyj, the great director of Armenian origin Serhij Paradžanov (1924-1990), who had close links with Ukraine, decided to turn the novel into a memorable film that conveys fully the chromaticism and symbolism of the book. The film was praised by critics around the world and is still remarkably relevant, although it is, of course, a different work from the original prose; for example, the neo-mythological appearance of the novel is almost entirely absent in the screenplay for the film, which operates interpolations and interpretations, often realistic and not numinous, in some crucial stages of the plot (for example, the fact that Marička was pregnant, which in the book is not declared, or the death of Ivan's brother, because he was saving him etc.). In Paradžanov, the cultural and anthropological perspective prevails, rather than the neo-mythological one. The figures of the *njavka*, the *čuhajstyr* and the *ščeznyk*, are absent from the film, because of the technical difficulties involved in transposing the numinosity onto film - with the consequent risk of falling into a parody of the horror genre.

In any case, his attempt to convey the novelist's intimate description of the natural environment of Hucul'ščyna led Paradžanov to illustrate the film from multiple perspectives, both those of the human protagonists and those of the natural elements, that is, "the wind, the flowers, even the water"[36]. For example, in the first scene, when Ivan's brother dies **crushed by** the tree he was felling, in an attempt to save Ivan from being crushed.

In the film, shot in the Carpathian Mountains, there is above all the visual enhancement of the colorful Hucul material culture[37]. Symbolism and ancestralism are illustrated by Paradžanov with unusual and interesting film techniques that represent, according Efird, "one of the most perplexing cinematic anomalies ever to reach the Soviet screen". In the scene of Ivan's father›s assassination, "although we first see Ivan's father Onufrii approaching, there is an abrupt shift into his line of vision as the latter raises and then strikes with his axe. Blood pours over the lens and the room begins to sway, finally cutting away to an oneiric image of red horses"[38].

Anyway, Steffen emphasizes that "this does not suggest that Parajanov somehow neglects the conventional virtues of the mise-en-scène; Ivan and Palahna's wedding illustrates the extent to which he consolidated his skills as director"[39].

---

36 Efird 2014, p. 24.
37 Steffen 2013, pp. 69-70.
38 Efird 2014, p. 27.
39 Steffen 2013, p. 70

BIBLIOGRAPHY

S. Andrusiv, "Adaptacija hucul's'koho mytu v povisti M. Kocjubyns'koho «Tini zabutych predkiv» ta romani-epopeï S. Vincenza «Na vysokij polonyni»" ["The Adaptation of the Hucul's Mythology in M. Kocjubyns'kyj's Novel «Shadows of Forgotten Ancestors» and in S. Vincenz's Epic Novel «In the Upper Valley»"], *Teka Komisji: polsko-ukrainskich związkow kulturowych*, vol. I, Lublin 2004, pp. 29-37.

I. Bestjuk, "Svojeridnist' transformaciï mifiv v hucul's'kij p"jesi H. Chotkevyča «Neproste» ta povisti M. Kocjubyns'koho «Tini zabutych predkiv»" ["A Different Transformation of the Hucul's Myths in H. Chotkevyč's Play «Uneasy» and in M. Kocjubyns'kyj's Novel «Shadows of Forgotten Ancestors»"], *Berdjans'kyj deržavnyj pedahohičnyj universytet. Zb. naukovych prac'*, 2006, n. 6, pp. 5-9.

L. Bilec'kyj, "«Tini zabutych predkiv» M. Kocjubyns'koho v svitli istoryčnoho rozvytku" ["M. Kocjubyns'kyj's «Shadows of Forgotten Ancestors» in Light of the Historical Evolution"], *Ukraïns'ke literaturoznavstvo*, n. 74, 2011, pp. 278-311 (first edition: 1933)

D.I. Čyževs'kyj, *Istorija ukraïns'koï literatury* [*History of Ukrainian Literature*], Kyïv 2003.

R. Efird, "Amorphous forms: time and subjectivity in *Shadows of Forgotten Ancestors*", *Studies in Russian and Soviet Cinema*, 8, 2014, n. 1, pp. 24-40.

V. Hnatjuk, *Znadoby do ukraïns'koï demonol'ohiï* [*Materials for Ukrainian Demonology*], L'viv 1912.

M. Kocjubyns'kyj, *Lysty do Volodymyra Hnatjuka* [*Letters to Volodymyr Hnatjuk*], L'viv 1914

M. Kocjubyns'kyj, *Tvory v semy tomach* [*Works in Seven Volumes*], vol. II, Kyïv 1974a.

M. Kocjubyns'kyj, *Tvory v semy tomach*, vol. III, Kyïv1974b.

M. Kocjubyns'kyj, *Tvory v semy tomach*, vol. V, Kyïv1974c.

M. Kocjubyns'kyj, *Tvory v semy tomach*, vol. VI, Kyïv 1975a.

M. Kocjubyns'kyj, *Tvory v semy tomach*, vol. VII, Kyïv 1975b.

M. Kocjubyns'kyj, *Lysty do Oleksandry Aplaksinoï* [*Letters to Aleksandra Aplaksina*], Kyïv 2008.

M. Laslo-Kucjuk, *Ključ do beletrystyky* [*A Key to the Belles Lettres*], Bucarest 2000.

O. Pachlovska, *Civiltà letteraria ucraina*, Rome 1998.

M. Potupejko (ed.), *Spohady pro Mychajla Kocjubyns'koho* [*Memoirs of Mychajlo Kocjubyns'kyj*], Kyïv 1962.

B. Rubchak, "The Music of Satan and the Bedeviled World: An Essay on Mykhailo Kotsiubynsky", in M. Kotsiubynsky, *Shadows of Forgotten Ancestors*, Littleton, Col., 1981.

O. Salij, "Ivan Franko ta Mychajlo Kocjubyns'kyj: dualistyčna koncepcija svitu. Dyscurs mistyčnoho (za povistju «Tini zabutych predkiv» i opovidannjamy «Jak Jura Šykmanjuk briv Čeremoš», «Teren u nozi»)" [Ivan Franko and Mychajlo Kocjubyns'kyj: Dualistic Conception of the World. Mystical Speech (in the novel «Shadows of Forgotten Ancestors» and in the tales «As Jura Šykmanjuk crossed the Čeremoš», «The Thorn in the Foot»)"], *Pytannja literaturoznavstva: naukovyj zbirnyk – Černivec'kyj nacional'nyj Universytet*, 82, 2011, pp. 190-199.

I. Siundiukov, "The socio-esthetic ideal through the eyes of Mykhailo Kotsiubynsky", in *Den'*, n. 38, 2002.

J. Steffen, *The Cinema of Sergei Parajanov*, Madison, Wisc. 2013.

D.H. Struk, *Mykhailo Kotsiubyns'kyi: The Modernist Prose Writer*, unpublished manuscript (available on the website of the University of Toronto).

F. Štejnbuk, "Povist' Mychajla Kocjubyns'koho «Tini zabutych predkiv» u konteksti tilesno-mimetyčnoho metodu analizu chudožnich tvoriv", ["Mychajlo Kocjubyns'kyj's Novel «Shadows of Forgotten Ancestors» within the Context of the Body-Mimetic Method of Analysis of Artistic Works"], *Studia Methodologica*, 30, 2010, pp. 241-246.

Korenizacija *as an ambiguous strategy of legitimization of Soviet power in Ukraine (1923-1933)*

*The article appeared, in an amendend form, in "History of Communism in Europe",
5, 2014.*

1. In 1923, a resolution of the Twelfth Soviet Communist Party Congress, accompanied by a resolution of the Party Central Committee, enforced the implementation of policies promoting national languages and national elites. These policies of enhancement of the nationalities, eventually called *korenizacija* ("taking root", indigenization), were enforced in order to attract the nationalities that were part of the Russian Empire; but this was not an official designation: Stalin always used the general term *nacionalizacija* and in Ukraine the term *Ukrainizacija* was preferred. The aim of this policy was to "make Soviet power seem 'native', 'intimate', 'popular', 'comprehensible'",[1] thanks to the use of native languages and the action of native cadres. Economic equalization, infrastructures, technology and cultural development were the objectives underlying *korenizacija*, especially in the most backward regions of the former Tsarist Empire (or regarded as such by the new Bolshevik power). Thus Soviet power undertook an ambitious but also ambiguous policy (for the suspicion that the Bolshevik internationalist culture anyway had towards nationalism) of aiding minority cultures, educating local cadres (also by liberalizing attendance of the best Russian universities), as well as protecting and encouraging the use of national languages.

---

1 Martin 2001, pp. 12.

It was a policy that rejected the principle of non-territorial national-cultural autonomy, developed by the Austromarxists and applied in the independent Ukrainian Rada's brief stint (1917-1918), whereas in the USSR national federated Republics were created and, within them, territories and autonomous districts for internal national minorities. National or local languages were the official languages of each Republic and autonomous territory, according to the idea that it was necessary to maximize the national cultures, depriving them of their separatist and non-Socialist content. Stalin then coined the phrase: "socialist in content and national in form"[2]. So the USSR "was the world's first state to institutionalize ethno-territorial federalism, classify all citizens according to their biological nationalities and formally prescribe preferential treatment of certain ethnically defined populations"[3].

Indeed, the Soviet government has shown evidence of poor linearity in its policies towards nationalities. Not only does this policy appears to have been contradictory in several spheres, but has undergone changes and transformations over the years, so as to make it almost unreadable. The ambiguity stems from the fact that it was also a sort of instrumental decolonization, which served to preserve the territorial boundaries and the amplitude of the Russian Empire so as not to give rise to centrifugal nationalisms, and the process of nation-building of the Empire's peoples was promoted[4]. In addition, it was hoped that an attraction would be exercised in the long term on those territories of Poland, Romania and Finland where strong Ukrainian (seven million people), Belarusian, Finnish and Romanian minorities lived: the Piedmont Principle[5].

The aim of *korenizacija* was also to categorize and control the population, according to a typical perspective of colonial power: "Soviet experts, like their British and German contemporaries, used their expertise to place their subjects into standardized knowable categories (…) that facilitated centralized rule"[6]. For a revolutionary power, social control also had a mobilizing role, which was to involve the Soviet peoples who had previously lived in the former Tsarist Empire in the socialist experiment. Therefore, "no issue was more central to the

---

2 *XVI s"ezd VKP/b* 1930, p. 56.
3 Slezkine 1994, p. 415.
4 Martin 2001, p. 1.
5 *Visti VUCVK* 10.4.1924, p. 1.
6 Hirsch 2005, p. 102.

formation of the Soviet Union than the national question"[7]. From a strictly political point of view, Stalin favored *korenizacija* especially because it aided alliances with the local Bolshevik leaders, given also the centralist tendencies of Trockij and his other opponents (and the backing of Ukraine was crucial in this battle)[8]. As a "cultural technology of rule", *korenizacija* assimilated the Soviet Union's practices to those of the Western powers but differed significantly from the colonial policy of Tsarist Russia, which had fluctuated between Russification and tolerant submission (religious and cultural tolerance, as in Poland, Finland and many Asian regions)[9].

As an example of forced Russification by the Tsarist Empire we can cite precisely the prohibition of public use of the Ukrainian language, which was in force between 1863 (the year of the Polish anti-tsarist uprising) and the 1905 Revolution in that part of Ukraine under Russian rule.

Indeed, as the renowned historian of British colonial rule, Nicholas Dirks, stressed, census-taking and border-making were forms of knowledge that "both enabled conquest and were produced by it; (…) knowledge was what colonialism was all about"[10]; cultural cataloging favored then a process of assimilation of peoples dominated, who, assuming the ruler's geo-cultural knowledge, were so ready to share their general culture. On the other hand, its revolutionary nature and a need for legitimacy through ethnic monitoring led the Soviet government to establish close contacts and connections with all ethnic groups of the USSR, unlike the British or French Empires, where only a few national groups had cultural and political links with the center[11].

According to Terry Martin, another element that allows us to understand the complexity of Soviet national policy lies in the fact that it was a soft-line policy, which served to make the hard-line policies acceptable (collectivization, industrialization, etc.): "this did not mean that the policy was insincere or purely decorative, but simply that it a was secondary consideration and would be implemented only to the extent it did not conflict with hard-line policy goals"[12].

---

7 *Ibid.*, p. 5.
8 Martin 2001, p. 84.
9 Hirsch 2005, p. 147.
10 Dirks 1996, p. IX.
11 Blitstein 2006, p. 288.
12 Martin 2001, p. 21.

Often the two approaches have coexisted and their apparent contradiction is explained by their different levels of importance, so that the party officials with their soft-line policies were obliged to continue to implement them while taking into account the signals coming from developments in the hard-line policies (especially repressive ones). According to Francine Hirsch, the difference between the regime's short-term goals and long-term goals should also be considered: from an initial differentiating themselves from colonialism and imperialist and "welcoming" the peoples in the new regime, to a fostering of the evolution of nations and ethnic groups in national socialist cultures, ready to converge in a ready-made communist state[13].

The contradictory nature of the Soviet nationalities policy is also explained by the modernist prejudices of the Bolsheviks, for which classifying and providing populations with a sense of nation meant setting them a step forward in the direction of their historical development (the Bolshevik leader Mikojan said therefore in 1925 that they were "creating and organizing new nations")[14]. Often it was precisely the demands of ethnographers, party officials and people conducting the surveys that guided individuals' choices; in this way many individuals somehow learned national distinctions which before were unknown to them.[15] This happened especially in areas such as western Ukraine, where coexistence between communities of different origin had much weakened ethnic barriers.

Anxiety over making classifications and modernistic prejudices made the border peasants seem treacherous in the eyes of the Bolshevik officials, who believed that ignorance and religion made them incapable of self-determination and subject to being manipulated by the "counter-revolution" and by foreign powers: promoting national culture and deporting members of minority came to be part of the same design for the remediation of boundaries[16]. However, in the early Thirties, the Bolshevik efforts towards classification obtained the desired effect: the majority of the population recognized themselves in the principle of national identification, while the Census consultants of 1926 had noted that they were often linked to localist identification criteria[17].

---

13 Hirsch 2005, pp. 8-9.
14 In Aliev 1926, p. 9.
15 Hirsch 2005, p. 14.
16 Brown 2003, p. 87.
17 Hirsch 2005, p. 145.

In general, the linguistic policies of *korenizacija* were successful in the West during the Twenties, but suffered a violent stop in the early Thirties; mostly for financial reasons, the opposite happened in the Soviet East, where there was a strong need for modernization; here, while many local cadres were actually promoted to top political position the problem of the formation of a sufficient number of technical cadres, remained unsolved.[18] Ukraine played a key role in *korenizacija*, due to its strategic position in economic and geopolitical terms and the sheer size of the country. In many regards, *korenizacija* is still considered a "golden age" of Ukrainian culture and language, and its ambiguity and tragic end are little known.

2. The failure of two Bolshevik regimes introduced in Ukraine in 1918 and in 1919 led Bolsheviks to understand that they had to recognize that Ukraine was a separate country.[19] A Bolshevik goal was even to create a link between the Russian-speaking cities and the countryside (where Ukrainians were the great majority), in order to better manage the Ukrainian agricultural resources[20].

In March 1920 Moscow had agreed to the entry of the Borot'bysty[21] (who were a faction of the Ukrainian Party of Socialist Revolutionaries) in the Ukrainian Communist Party after the Eighth Congress approved Lenin's strategic document "On Soviet Rule in Ukraine" and after the publication of a "Letter to the Workers and peasants of Ukraine" of December 28, 1919 which announced that the Borot'bysty would have a significant role in Ukrainian communism[22]; in a proclamation to the Red Army, Trockij even declared that "only the Ukrainian worker and peasant possess the sole right to rule their own country"[23].

However, the Soviet Constitution of 1924 gave the centre many powers although Stalin's proposal to federate the national Republics (including Ukraine) in the Russian Republic had been shelved, and the Soviet Republic had the same powers as the Russian regions, while the party remained centralized. The use of national languages in the

---

18 Martin 2001, pp. 25-26.
19 Mace 1983, p. 40.
20 Liber 1992, p. 46.
21 Mace 1983, p. 62.
22 Lenin 1959, pp. 403-410.
23 Vynnyčenko 1920, pp. 494-495.

educational system was favored, but not in the Universities. The central Soviet government worked in Russian. In Ukraine, the Bolshevik Party was dominated by the Russians and it was thanks to Lenin - who rejected the proposal - that the emergence of an autonomous Republic in the Donbas was prevented. Eighty per cent of the members of the KP(b)U (Communist Party of Ukraine) and 95% of government officials were Russians or Russified[24]. In 1921 the head of the Ukrainian Soviet government, the Bolshevik of Bulgarian origin Christian Rakovskij (who, however, in 1923, to escape the control of Moscow, criticized Soviet centralism), stated that "the triumph of the Ukrainian language would mean the rule of the Ukrainian petit-bourgeois intelligentsia and the Ukrainian kulaks"[25]. In March 1923 Dmitrij Lebed', the second secretary of the Central Committee of the KP(b)U spoke of "two cultures" locked in a deadly struggle: the reactionary Ukrainian culture and that of the Russian Bolsheviks[26].

The period 1923-1925 was that of "Ukrainization by decree", which favored the use of the Ukrainian language in all areas and the access of Ukrainians to state and party jobs; bilingualism was imposed on officials and courses of Ukrainian were set up for civil servants. The first decree was issued by the Central Committee of the KP(b)U on June 22, 1923[27]. On July 16, 1923 the Ukrainian Vlas Čubar replaced Rakovskij as chairman of the Ukrainian government. Between 1924 and 1929 29 national districts were also created in Ukraine: 7 German, 4 Bulgarian, 3 Greek, 1 Polish, and 2 Jewish; the 9 Russian districts were only introduced in 1927. There were also 66 Jewish and (from 1928) 41 Russian national cities, as well as a thousand Soviet national villages[28].

The leaders of the KP(b)U, Emmanuel Kviring (an ethnic German, who had been in favor of the secession of the Donbas) and his deputy Lebed' (a Russian), were still hostile to *korenizacija*; among civil servants who were party members, only 18% knew Ukrainian, while only 15% of those enrolled concluded the semi-compulsory Ukrainian language courses. Only 10-15% of the documen-

---

24 Liber 1992, p. 12.
25 RSASPH 17, 26, 1.
26 Lebed' 1923, p. 1.
27 *Kul'turne budivnyctvo* 1929, pp. 229-232
28 Martin 2001, p. 40. See also Brown 2003.

tation of the government was in Ukrainian[29]. There were, however, developments in primary education and in the press in Ukrainian.

To strengthen Ukrainization, in March of 1925 Kaganovič was sent to Ukraine by Stalin - as part of his policy of alliance with nationalism - as the first secretary of the KP(b)U. He created a special office of the Party for the Ukrainization, which was developed in all fields, even in the use of movie subtitles. Between 1925 and 1928 there was almost a doubling of the percentage of the press, and 65% of publications in Ukrainian, while books in Ukrainian increased from 40 to 54% of total publications. Areas in which developments were minor were oral communication, the environment of managers and "specialists", and the Komsomol, while passive resistance and resentment on the part of the Russians remained the main problem[30]. Urban workers (most of them Russian speakers), state and party officials, industrial specialists, branches of all-union enterprises were those who were opposed to the linguistic *korenizacija*. Stalin did not subject trade unions and industrial workers to the policy of forced Ukrainization; he saw Ukrainization as a social policy primarily to acquire the consent of the Ukrainian peasant world but he was afraid of losing control of the Donbas, where the Ukrainian industrial proletariat (mostly Russophone) was concentrated.

3. But already in 1926 a turnaround took place, also caused by the return to power of Piłsudski in Poland and by fears of a new Polish-Ukrainian alliance. The first official expression of the "Russian question" in Ukraine was proposed in 1926 by Jurij Larin, a representative of Komzet (Committee for the Settlement of Working Jews on the Land) in the Central Executive Committee of the Soviet Union (the Soviet of Nationalities was one of its two chambers), backed by Enukidze, the secretary of the Central Executive Committee[31]. The majority of party members were by then opposed to *korenizacija*. On the other hand, opposition to *korenizacija* was condemned by the organs of the party and of the state, but without resort to serious measures such as arrest and execution[32].

---

29 RSASPH 17, 85, 4.
30 Martin 2001, pp. 92-95.
31 *Vtoraja sessija CIK SSSR* 1926, p. 460-500.
32 Martin 2001, p. 76.

In March 1926, a major controversy broke out within the KP(b) U on the sensitive issue of the industrial proletariat; Šums'kyj, the Ukrainian Commissioner for Education, strongly criticized the position taken by Kaganovič, according to which the proletariat were not to be forcibly Ukrainized. The controversy was also an opportunity for the Ukrainian communists to have direct access to political power in the party and get rid of Kaganovič, as in 1925 Kviring had been dismissed. Previously Šums'kyj had asked Stalin to replace Kaganovič to with a Ukrainian leader[33]. Šums'kyj's request, however, was inconsistent with a rule imposed by Stalin, which - in order to avoid an excess of nationalism - stated that the position of secretary of the national Parties (with the exception of Georgia and Armenia) should be held by leaders of non-national origin, while the leadership of state bodies was entrusted to members of their own national exponents[34]. In fact, until June 1953, the First Secretary of the Ukrainian Party wasn't a Ukrainian.

Kaganovič's self-defense before Stalin was a success, mainly because of two sensitive issues: Šums'kyj was a Borot'byst and was now being accused of wanting to reconstitute that group inside the Bolshevik Party; moreover, Kaganovič brought to Stalin's attention the brilliant young Ukrainian writer Mykola Chvyl'ovyj who advocated the Ukrainization of the proletariat and the de-Russification of Ukrainian literature, suggesting that a dangerously anti-Soviet chauvinism was gaining ground in Ukraine[35]. Stalin, in his reply addressed to the Ukrainian Central Committee, rejected the idea of a "Ukrainization of the proletariat from above" and condemned "Chvyl'ovyj 's anti-muscovite extremism", while "the West European proletariats are full of sympathy towards Moscow as a citadel of the International proletarian movement and Leninism"[36].

In June of 1926, strong in his political victory, Kaganovič read out a proud report to the Central Committee: "On the Results of Ukrainization", which outlined the correct ideological foundations (that guided Ukrainian *korenizacija* in subsequent years), according to which Ukrainization was a weapon to fight Russian and Ukrainian nationalism, while it would have been unaccept-

---

33 Radziejowski 1983, p. 118.
34 *Tajny nacional'noj politiki CK RKP* 1992, p. 83.
35 RSASPH, 558, 11, 738.
36 The letter was published in Stalin 1934.

able to oppose Ukrainian culture to any other culture of the peoples that made up the USSR; on the other hand he appreciated the efforts to promote knowledge of the Ukrainian language by those workers who had been previously Russified and spoke a mixed Russian-Ukrainian dialect (*suržyk*), but did not accept the excesses of those who wanted a total Ukrainization of the workers. Kaganovič then highlighted the successes of *korenizacija*: the amount of state documentation in the Ukrainian had increased from 20 to 65%, the Ukrainian press had reached 60% of the total, while there had been significant developments in education and in the presence of Ukrainian party members (which was now 47%, with a peak of 61% in the Komsomol)[37].

In March 1927 Šums'kyj was deposed (in 1933 he was arrested and exiled in Siberia and died, poisoned, in 1946); as Trockij had not yet been defeated, Skrypnyk, one of the few old Bolshevik leaders who was Ukrainian was appointed in his place. In 1928 the Communist Party of Ukraine declared that Šums'kysm and Chvyl'ovysm were the doctrines of Ukrainian fascism[38]. It was the end of the two roots theory of Ukrainian communism, Bolshevik and Borot'byst, which had also marked the first official history of the party, written in 1923 by Moisej Ravič-Čerkasskij[39]. Chvyl'ovyj committed suicide in May 1933.

An appendix of the clash between Šums'kyj and Kaganovič was the position taken by the economist of Russian origin Mychajlo Volobujev, who was an official of the Ukrainian Commissariat for Education, and who published in 1928 an article on the organ of the Communist Party (*Bil'šovyk Ukraïny*) in which he demonstrated the existence of an unequal exchange between Ukraine and Russia, which showed a continuity between the Tsarist and Soviet eras in the colonial exploitation of Ukraine; he put forward a series of proposals for favoring the self-management of the economy of Ukraine (Ukrainian full control on the national economy, curtailment of the powers of the State Planning Commission, exceeding of Russo-centric Soviet industrial planning, etc.)[40]. Criticism of Volobujev's thesis was violent, and Skryp-

<hr>

37 *Budivnyctvo Radjans'koï Ukraïny* 1928, pp. 58-65.
38 RSASPH, 17, 26, 15.
39 M. Ravič-Čerkasskij 1923, p. 165.
40 Volobujev 1962, pp. 228-229.

nyk, likening Volobujev to Šums'kyj and Chvyl'ovyj, stated that "this *petite bourgeoisie*, ideologically fascist, says that we have a Ukrainian colony in the Union"[41]. In the spring of 1930 Volobujev was forced to write a humiliating recantation entitled "Towards a Critique of Volobujevism"[42].

4. Skrypnyk was Lenin's man in Ukraine and participated in the Bolshevik Ukrainian governments during the Civil War; he represented Ukraine in the Soviet of Nationalities and in 1926 had established for himself a chair of Studies on nationality in the Ukrainian Institute of Marxism-Leninism. After 1927 he became the most important political figure in Ukraine, despite the appointment in 1928 as First Secretary of Kosior (a Pole from Donbas, who never learned Ukrainian)[43], in place of Kaganovič. Indeed, after the replacement of Kaganovič, which Stalin agreed to in exchange for Skrypnyk's support in the fight against Bucharin, "he came to see himself as a virtually independent national leader"[44]. From the theoretical point of view, Skrypnyk thought of Ukraine as "a large social laboratory for the Leninist solution of the National question"[45].

Skrypnyk implemented *korenizacija* and tried to extend it to those areas that were unaffected. It increased the number of Ukrainians living in cities: according to the 1897 census, Ukrainians accounted for only 32.5% of the urban population, which decreased to 15.9% for cities with more than 100,000 inhabitants. The Russians accounted for 33.7% of the total urban population and the Jews 27.4%. Already in 1926 the Ukrainians represented 47% of the urban population (33% of those with more than 100,000 inhabitants)[46]. The number of Ukrainian immigrants in the industrial cities (Donbas and south-eastern Ukraine) also increased: in 1933 Ukrainians accounted for almost half or more of the inhabitants in Luhans'k, Zaporižžja, Charkiv and Dnipropetrovs'k; only in Stalino (now Donec'k), they accounted for 31% of the population (but in 1923 they were only 7%

---

41 Skrypnyk 1928, p. 46.
42 Volobujev 1930.
43 Majstrenko 1985, p. 227-228.
44 Mace 1983, p. 304.
45 Skrypnyk 1974, p. 380.
46 *Korotki pidsumky* 1926, pp. 204-209.

of the population)[47]. As a result, the Ukrainians became the majority of industrial workers: in 1934 they far exceeded 60% of the total[48]. For industrial workers, however, there were no required courses and Ukrainian immigrants from the countryside accepted the dominance of the Russian language in the factories: although increased compared to 1926, in 1929, only 32% of industrial workers used Ukrainian in conversation[49].

On the other hand, one of the most important effects of *korenizacija* was that a number of Russified workers began to identify with the Ukrainian nationality and many urbanized Ukrainians passed from forms of regional identity to identify with the Ukrainian national identity, which they encountered for the first time. In many respects, it was an intended strategy pursued by the policy of Skrypnyk (according to an idea already put forward by Stalin), who had theorized a parallel with what had already happened in the Czech cities of the nineteenth century with German culture[50].

However, the growing Ukrainization of the cities and the use of Ukrainian in entertainment, in the media and in collective activities, reversed the previous trend which made of them a vehicle for Russification; but it was an uneven process that varied depending on the region, the city, the proximity to Russia, jobs and trades[51]. In general, "the Ukrainization of the proletariat, then, appeared to be moving in the direction of a territorial Ukrainian identity that was bilingual and open to both ethnic Ukrainians and Russians"[52].

The action of Skrypnyk in the field of education led to results: in 1930, Ukrainian schools were attended by almost all Ukrainian-speaking children and about 20% of Russian-speaking[53]. The percentage of publications in Ukrainian increased, but the same Skrypnyk noted that in 1929 only 15% of the literature was sold in the Ukrainian language[54]. On the other hand, in August 1929, it was possible to Ukrainize the newspaper of Odesa and get good results

47 Liber 1992, p. 57.
48 Asatkin 1935, p. 386.
49 Liber 1992, pp. 82-83.
50 Skrypnyk 1928, p. 18.
51 Liber 1992, pp. 110-112.
52 Martin 2001, p. 105.
53 Skrypnyk 2005.
54 SARF 374, 27s, 1709.

in the Ukrainization of the city[55]; before the war, only 6% of Odesa's inhabitants were Ukrainians, which fell to 3% in 1920[56]. These figures should be seen in relation to others of a clearly opposite nature: in 1929, a decree (not published) of the Presidium of the Central Executive Committee of the Soviet Union established that the internal documents of filials of all-unions institutions, could be written in Russian[57]; in this way all previous efforts of Ukrainization of non-local companies were thwarted. Public transport also suffered from the tendency to restore Russian and, for example, in 1931, all Ukrainian insignia in Charkiv station were eliminated[58]. From 1928 on, the work of the Party Committee for Ukrainization practically ceased, while dismissals due to resistance to the use of the Ukrainian language became very rare - in 1927 there had been several hundred[59]. According to Terry Martin, Ukrainization led to a kind of bilingualism, with the dominance of Russian in the economic and industrial fields, and of Ukrainian in political and cultural life, in rural areas and in the soft-line political spheres[60].

In 1926 there was also the decision on the part of Kaganovič to set up a secret commission on the activities of Ukrainian intellectuals[61], many of whom, like Hruševs'kyj, had agreed to return to Soviet Ukraine and do their job in the service of cultural *korenizacija*. Thus started a policy contrary to *korenizacija*, which grew over time and had the GPU as protagonist with its reports on the activities of the "chauvinist circles"[62]. At the end of 1928 the first explicit Russian interference in the cultural life of Ukraine also began, with the attack by the secretary of the All-Union Society of Marxist Historians, Pavel Gorin, on the Marxist historian Matvij Javors'kyj, the chief representative in Ukraine of the regime's historiography; the accusation, also published in *Pravda* on February 10, 1929, was that Javors'kyj overestimated the national historic factor and treated the history of Ukraine separately from the general historical dynamics[63].

---

55 Skrypnyk 1974, pp. 142-145
56 *Mis'ki selyšča USSR*, pp. 2-17.
57 SARF, P3316, 24, 643.
58 CSAPOU 1, 20, 4172.
59 Martin 2001, p. 119-120.
60 *Ibid.*, pp. 122-123.
61 CSAPOU, 1, 6, 102.
62 Martin 2001, p. 225.
63 Plokhy 2005, pp. 383-397.

Even Skrypnyk eventually had to take a stand against Javors'kyj and in June 1931 the entire Ukrainian Institute of Marxism-Leninism, where Skrypnyk also taught, was dissolved.

Collectivization and industrialization were then mechanisms objectively contrary to the national principle and to *korenizacija*, because they strengthened economic planning based on non-national economic regions and affected the territory which had been segmented into National districts and villages[64]. Nevertheless, Stalin continued to attack the internationalist positions and confirmed several times the *korenizacija* line. In June 1930 at the Sixteenth Party Congress, he stated that indeed "the construction of socialism in the USSR is the period of the flowering of national culture"[65]. In Stalin's speech, Russian chauvinism and internationalism were identified, probably in the context of the fight against "specialists" - i.e. engineers and scientists trained in Tsarist era - that the regime had been conducting since the NEP had been liquidated.

Defense of *korenizacija* was however associated, in the words of Stalin, with a most intense fight against nationalism. In the previous months, several show trials were held against groups of intellectuals in Ukraine, Belarus and other Republics or national regions. The most publicized trial was the Ukrainian one, organized against some of the leading Ukrainian intellectuals accused of having founded a mysterious independent organization (SVU, Union for the Liberation of Ukraine). It was intended, too, as a clear signal to Poland on the intention on the part of the Soviet power to eliminate all possible support in Ukraine for Polish ambitions. Starting in July of 1929, with the arrest of Serhij Jefremov (the most prominent Ukrainian literary critic), with the SVU show trial, a decade of harsh repression began; in 1930 the Ukrainian Autocephalous Orthodox Church, accused of Petljurism[66], was also suppressed.

Since 1926, the GPU, as mentioned, had judged the political and cultural situation in Ukraine to be dangerous. In May 1928 the Politburo of the KP(b)U had ordered to investigation into Jefremov and the entire Ukrainian intelligentsia[67]. The show trial against the Union for the Liberation of Ukraine was then part of the struggle against

---

64 Martin 2001,pp. 243-244.
65 *XVI s"ezd* 1930, p. 56.
66 Bociurkiw 1979-80, p. 8.
67 CSAPOU 1, 16, 6.

the "specialists" hired by the regime (so, perhaps, Skrypnyk interpreted it), but was also uniquely Ukrainian. Of the 45 accused, there were Autocephalous priests, two historians, 3 linguists, 3 medical researchers, several academics, teachers, professors and activists of rural cooperatives[68]. "The trial was also a blow aimed at Skrypnyk, just as the Shakty affair had been directed against Bukharin"[69].

The SVU trial showed, indirectly, the growth of a Soviet xenophobia, which was primarily ideological and not, as tsarist xenophobia had been, ethnic, but it had also inherited something of the latter. Great importance was given, in this context, to the Special Administrative Regions of the border. In Ukraine, 2-3 million people, mostly Poles, Germans and Ukrainians lived in these regions. Fears of a wave of emigration of Poles from Ukraine led therefore to the first ethnic Soviet deportation, after the mass demonstrations of February 1930 in the border regions of Ukraine against collectivization. The Politburo's decree of deportation hit "in the first line, those of Polish nationality"[70]. A new phase began in the Soviet nationalities policy, which targeted "non-Soviet" nationalities, i.e. those that had their own homeland outside the borders of the USSR, and therefore also qualified as "enemy nations".

5. Though Stalin in 1930 had attacked Russian chauvinism, at the end of that same year he began to reevaluate in his writings the tradition of the Russian state, according to a line that, in the mid-Thirties, led the Soviet regime to place Russian nationality at the center of political discourse. For example, in a letter of December 1930, he wrote to Dem'jan Bednyj: "the <u>Russian</u> working class is the advance-guard of the Soviet workers" while strongly criticizing the negative treatment Bednyj reserved to the historical Russian past[71].

Several factors pushed in this direction: economic centralization strengthened the existing Russian state tradition, and in 1927 the Ukrainian government controlled about 80% of the Ukrainian industry, a share which in 1932 had dropped drastically to 37.5%[72]. On the other hand, collectivization met with the greatest resistance in

---

68 *Visti VUCVK* 11 Mars 1930, p. 3.
69 Mace 1983, p. 276.
70 RSASPH 17, 162, 8.
71 Stalin 1953, pp. 24-25.
72 Holubnychy 1982, p. 818.

Ukraine and the other non-Russian Republics. After defeating his opponents at home, Stalin became more sensitive to the dangers linked to the resentment of Russian speakers towards Ukrainization, which he began to see as encouraging dangerous nationalist, anti-centralist, pro-Western tendencies[73]. The majority of Russian speakers were in fact hostile and cold towards Ukrainization, especially for the language; a worker complained, for example, in 1926: "they made me an illiterate person from a literate one"[74]. In a speech of 1933, a senior member of the KP(b)U complained that there were not a few cases of Russian officials dismissed because they refused or were unable to learn Ukrainian[75].

Another factor that led to the crisis of *korenizacija* was represented by requests to extend Ukrainization to the large Ukrainian minority in Russia and in the Kuban', associated with claims for territorial changes in favor of the Republic of Ukraine, as had already taken place between 1924 and 1926 for Belarus, which had increased its population by two million inhabitants (many were Russians). Ukraine had instead had to cede eastern Donbas and the region of Taganrog on the Azov Sea, receiving in the north (in the regions of Kursk and Voronež) only half of the Russian territory inhabited by Ukrainians; this was the only case in which the territorial modifications did not penalize the territory of the Russian Republic. The subsequent pressure to prevent the Russification of nearly eight million of Ukrainians living in the Russian republic (census 1926), led, at the end of 1928, to the beginning of a vast campaign of Ukrainization of Ukrainians of Russia spurred by the Soviet of Nationalities of the Central Committee[76].

The outbreak of the serious issue of grain requisitions eventually led to the final turning against Ukrainization. In March of 1928, Kaganovič had already associated, in a speech at the plenum of the Central Committee of the Communist Party, nationalism with resistance to grain requisitions.[77] Korenizacija's formal cancellation in Ukraine was ratified by two secret decrees of the central Politbjuro of 14 and 15 December, 1932, at the height of the campaign of grain requisitioning. The Politbjuro issued the decrees after the return of Molotov

---

73 Martin 2001, pp. 271-273.
74 *Bol'ševik*, n. 23-24, 31.12.1926, p. 55.
75 Ljubčenko 1933, p. 2.
76 Martin 2001, pp. 279-291.
77 RSASPH 17, 26, 15.

and Kaganovič, who had been sent to Ukraine and Kuban' to guide the operations of grain requisitioning. The decree of 14 December put in close connection with the severe agrarian crisis the "lack of vigilance" over Ukrainization, which had allowed "kulaks, former officers, Petljurites (…) to penetrate collective farm leadership"[78]. The decree did not abrogate Ukrainization altogether, but its "mechanical" application which was not assigned to "Bolshevik cadres." The decree of 15 December abolished Ukrainization in the Federal Russian Republic[79].

After the decrees of December 1932, a wave of repression began in Ukraine that struck the Ukrainian intelligentsia, the community of western Ukrainians (mostly members of the Communist Party), and the national-communists. The most important victim was Skrypnyk. Since January 1933 compulsory courses of Ukrainian culture in the Universities had been abolished. After months of criticism and arrests of his close associates, Skrypnyk committed suicide in July 1933. At the XVII Party Congress Stalin drew the consequences of all this: "the vestiges of capitalism are much more vital in the realm of nationalities policy than in any other"[80]. It was the tombstone on *korenizacija*, which continued in Ukraine but within very narrow limits, juxtaposed by repression and a growing appreciation of Russian culture.

Ukrainization however had achieved significant results. For example, in 1930, almost 90% of all primary school students were enrolled in Ukrainain-language schools; 60% of industrial and technical schools were Ukrainized;[81] according to a 1933 survey of the new Education Commissar, Zatons'kyj, only half of Russian-speaking children attended a Russian school in Ukraine[82]. The Ukrainian members of the Communist Party had grown significantly, from 23% in 1922 to 60% in October 1933; yet, less sustained growth took place in the presence of Ukrainians in the Central Committee, increasing from 16% in 1924 to 43% in 1930. Finally, many members of the party claimed to be Russian-speaking Ukrainians (in 1927 it was almost 40% of registered Ukrainian), which made the Ukrain-

<hr>

78 RSASPH 17, 3, 911.
79 RSASPH 17, 3, 911.
80 *XVII s"ezd* 1934, p. 31.
81 *KP(b)U* 1930, p. 276.
82 CSASBPGU 539, 11, 1112.

130

ian speakers a minority in the Party[83]. On the other hand, the decrease in the numbers of Russians in the Party was a worry for Moscow because of the loyalty of the Ukrainian apparatus and the fidelity of Ukraine in case of war. What Stalin said explicitly in the famous letter to Kaganovič on 11 August 1932, the one that started the Stalinist attack to Ukraine:

The most important thing now is Ukraine. The current situation in Ukraine is terribly negative. *It is negative in the party.* (...) About 50 district committees have spoken out against the plan of stocking grain after judging it to be *unrealistic.* It is no longer a party, it is a parliament, a caricature of parliament. (...) Kosior was put in a corner. *Things go wrong with the Soviets.* Čubar is not a leader. *The situation is not good* with the OGPU. Redens is not leading the fight against the counter-revolutionaries in a republic so great and special as Ukraine. If we do not act immediately to resolve the situation in Ukraine, we risk losing Ukraine. Keep in mind that Pilsudski does not give up, his ability to spy in Ukraine is much greater than what Redens and Kosior understand. And remember also that in the Communist Party of Ukraine (500,000 members, ha ha!), there are quite a few (yes, quite a few!) rotten subjects, conscious or unconscious Petljurists and direct agents of Pilsudski. As soon as things get worse, these elements will waste no time before they open a front inside (and outside) the Party, against the Party[84].

The terrible winter of 1933 that followed brought heavy requisitions which caused a man-made famine in the Ukrainian countryside with millions of deaths: the Holodomor.

By November, 1933, thousands of office workers, teachers, academics were arrested or removed from their posts. There was condemnation of the introduction of the Ukranian alphabet brought about by Skrypnyk, in his important 1928 reform with standardization of spelling including the letter *g* already used in Galicia (to be used for the corresponding sound in foreign languages) and Kosior accused him of favoring the introduction into the Ukrainian lexicon of foreign words in place of Russian ones[85]; its spelling system (*Skrypnykivka*) was therefore abolished but remained in use in Galicia and in the Ukrainian diaspora[86]. After 1933, national-communism became a condemnable ideology, the ties between Ukraine and Russia were increasingly emphasized and, unlike before, the assimilation of nation-

---

83 Liber 1992, p. 82, p. 94, p. 226.
84 Published in Chlevnjuk 2001, p. 273-274.
85 Kosior 1933.
86 Mace 1983, p. 226.

al minorities was encouraged[87]. In those months, in addition, there was a wave of spontaneous de-Ukrainization, especially in the areas mostly inhabited by Russians: the journal of the province of Luhans'k came to be written in Russian, as the documents of the city government of Donec'k, and the University of Odesa began again to be Russian-speaking[88]. There was also a radical change in the percentage distribution of newspapers: if in 1932 90% of them were in Ukrainian and 4% in Russian, in 1938 the ratio went to 68-30% (and sometimes the content of newspapers was in Russian although the title was in Ukrainian)[89]. In December 1937 there was a decree of the Central Committee of the Party (Orgbjuro) that explicitly condemned as "incorrect and politically erroneous (…) the lack of newspaper in Russian" and ordered the creation of Russian newspapers in the major Ukrainian cities[90].

At the November 1933 KP(b)U plenum, Kosior and his deputy Postyšev (Stalin's emissary sent in January to lead the requisitioning of grain) stated that Ukraine was now a mature industrial nation, no longer threatened by the Russian chauvinism and that the greatest danger now was Ukrainian nationalism; a "Bolshevik Ukrainization" would still be brought forward by the party[91]. After 1933, "Bolshevik *korenizacija*" was much less linguistic and more given to promoting ethnically Ukrainian cadres in the State and Party[92]. There was also an effort to maintain and develop productive investment in the non-Russian Republics. The end of the original *korenizacija* provincialized Ukraine, which often found itself relating to the world through the mediation of Russian language and culture[93].

---

87 Martin 2001, p. 356.
88 CSAPOU 1, 1, 421; 1, 20, 6634.
89 Martin 2001, p. 369.
90 RSASPH 17, 114, 633; 17, 21, 4685.
91 *XII z"izd KP(b)U* 1934, p. 66-67.
92 Martin 2001, p. 367-368.
93 Szporluk 1979-1980, p. 846.

6. National repression in Ukraine and fears of an impending war were the main factors that led Stalin to launch, from the mid-Thirties, the Russo-centric politics of National Bolshevism, which was synthesized by the famous editorial in *Pravda* of February 1, 1936, which proclaimed the Russian people "first among equals" of the Soviet peoples. Along with the large decrease in *korenizacija*, there was a general change in the role played by Russia in the Soviet system, that "settled upon a Russo-centric form of etatism as most effective way to promote state-building and popular loyalty to the regime."[94] This was based on three perspectives: the Russification of the Russian Republic, the elevation of Russian culture to a unifying culture of the Soviet Union, the new rhetoric (Russian-centric) of the Friendship of the Peoples,[95] which was introduced by Stalin in December 1935 with the aim of shoring up the new Russian centrality while maintaining the multinational structure of the USSR[96]. On the other hand, in 1926, Russians accounted for 52% of the population of the USSR, they were the majority of the working class and 9 million of them living outside the Russian Republic, mostly concentrated in the most important non-Russian cities. They therefore constituted the main force on which to place a policy of strengthening the fortress which the USSR appeared to be turning into because of alleged threats of war from outside[97].

One of the consequences was that the percentage of those who declared themselves Ukrainian collapsed between the censuses of 1926 and of 1937: from 8 to 3 millions in the Russian Republic and from 4 million to 250 thousands in the North Caucasus and Kuban' (where repression and famine had been harsh); in general, national minorities in the Russian regions of the Russian Republic went down from 15 to 4%, while in the same regions in 1938 practically all non-Russian schools had been closed[98]. In the Thirties there was a strange phenomenon: the Soviet and Western colonial policies passed the baton; while the USSR walked toward the western colonial practices of exclusion, in the Western empires something akin to the Soviet policies

---

94 Brandenberger 2002, p. 2.
95 Martin 2001, p. 394.
96 *Ibid.*, p. 432.
97 Liber 1992, p. 148-152.
98 Martin 2001, p. 405-410.

of nazionalizing took place[99]. In the USSR, even the central institutions of the politics of nationality suffered a sharp decline, with the abolition of Nationalities Department of the Central Committee and the near cessation of the works of the Presidium of the Soviet of Nationalities. "This process led to the division of the Soviet Union into a central Russian core and a non-Russian 'national' periphery"[100]. Stalin's new Russocentrism, however, was more pragmatic than ideological and did not intend to encourage ethnic Russians, but to make accessible, shared and popular the political objectives of the regime by presenting them in forms of a Russian patriotism[101]. This is why *korenizacija* continued its course, albeit with the limitations described above.

Between 1935 and 1938, at least nine nationalities were affected by ethnic cleansing and classified as "enemy nations". Thus, the Great Terror had a close connection with the issue of nationality: the diaspora nations (who had their motherland outside the borders of the USSR) became enemy nations to decimate and deport, while Ukraine and Belarus were made bi-national and the Russian Federative Republic was Russified. Finally, traditional Russian culture, history, literature and language were placed at the center of Soviet life[102]. The Friendship of the Peoples' ideology was also a formula that loosened class solidarity linked to the previous classist metaphors and strengthened the wartime alliance between the Soviet peoples, around the Russian nucleus. In fact, Stalin said in a speech in 1935: "while this friendship exists, the peoples of our country will be free and unconquerable"[103]. This turn, according to Francine Hirsch, was however consistent with the long-term goal of a communist "evolution" and merging of the nations[104].

But the transition from the class to the people, together with the anxiety regarding national classification that had characterized the Soviet regime from the outset, according to Martin, produced from the end of the Thirties a crystallization of the concept of nation and the emergence of a primordial, semi-natural conception of its essence.

---

99 Blitstein 2006, p. 289-291.
100 Martin 2001, p. 412.
101 Brandenberger 2002, p. 4-5.
102 Martin 2001, p. 423.
103 *Pravda*, n. 335, 6.12.1935, p. 3.
104 Hirsch 2005, p. 9.

From the historicist conception that was typical of the national theory that animated *korenizacija*, Stalin passed to a semi-natural vision, which was associated with the opposite trend that pragmatically enabled and facilitated assimilation to the Russian nation of the minorities within the Russian Federative Republic or the minorities that populated regions and Republics (such as Ukraine) in which there was a Russian presence; this primordialism is also associated with the emerging category of "enemy nations"[105] and was greatly strengthened and made to look like racism (despite the fact that the Soviet regime made considerable efforts to fight ideologically biological determinism)[106] by the NKVD's Decree of 2 April 1938. This imposed on individuals the nationality of their parents[107]. This semi-racism was not, according to Martin, a deliberate project but the cumulative effect of a series of administrative and political trends in Soviet life[108]. Eric Weitz spoke of "racial politics without the overt concept and ideology of race"[109], similar (but with much more serious effects in the USSR) to what had happened in Western countries in the first half of the twentieth century, where eugenics, immigration policies and war internment promoted racist policies, albeit in liberal regimes[110].

7. The irreconcilable contradictions of *korenizacija* that Francine Hirsch defined "*by its nature* both a creative and a destructive process"[111], had de-Ukrainization effects after World War II. In 1958, an important educational reform desired by Chruščёv was launched, giving freedom of choice to parents about the language of the education of their children, and then forbidding in practice the individual Republics to impose their own language in schools, making a huge contribution to Russification: at the end of communism in Kyïv only 300,000 out of 790,000 pupils attended a Ukrainian school[112]. At the beginning of the seventies, with the emergence of the rhetoric of the Soviet people and Russian as a lingua franca, all Ukrainian dissidents were subjected to harsh repression with heavy prison sentences,

---

105 Martin 2001, p. 449-450.
106 Hirsch 2005, p. 231-271.
107 SARF 9401, 12, 37.
108 Martin 2001, p. 451.
109 Weitz 2002, p. 3.
110 Perri 2013.
111 Hirsch 2002, p. 42.
112 Subtelny 2102, p. 536.

or hard labor, and sometimes sent to asylums. The campaign of Russification under Brežnev had important results: the periodicals published in Ukrainian passed from 46 to 19% between 1969 and 1980, while books went down from 60 to 24% between 1958 and 1980. The share of Russian-speaking Ukrainians and those who were bilingual increased. Thus, Milan Kundera wrote in 1984: "One of the largest European countries (there are nearly forty million Ukrainians) is fast disappearing. And this huge, incredible event is happening without the world noticing it"[113].

8. Undoubtedly, it can be said that *korenizacija* represented an important milestone in the tortuous and dramatic process of Ukrainian nation-building. Not only that: *korenizacija* aided the historical recognition of the actual existence of a Ukrainian nation, the existence of which cannot now be seriously questioned by anyone, without falling into absurd anachronisms, like those who hark back to the ancient geographical Tsarist categories to justify today's questioning of the territorial integrity of Ukraine and of the entire post-Soviet space. On the other hand, *korenizacija*'s ambiguous character, which we have extensively documented, and its violent stop in Ukraine that took place in 1932, greatly diminish its importance for the development of Ukrainian culture. Indeed, in the Thirties, giving vent to what Sacharov also once called Stalin's ukrainophobia, the Soviet regime began the process of a widespread Russification of Ukraine which occurred mainly in the Brežnevian age. Moreover, as we have said, the end of *korenizacija* provincialized Ukraine for a long time.

---

113 Kundera 1984.

U. Aliev, *Nacional'nyj vopros i nacional'naja kul'tura* [*National Problem and National Culture*], Rostov-on-Don 1926.

O. Asatkin (ed.), *Narodne hospodarstvo USSR (Statystyčnyj dovidnyk)* [*National Economy of USSR. Statistical Handbook*], Kyïv 1935.

P.A. Blitstein, "Cultural Diversity and the Interwar Conjuncture: Soviet Nationality Policy in Its Comparative Context", *Slavic Review*, 2, 2006, pp. 273–93.

B.R. Bociurkiw, "Ukrainization Movements Within the Russian Orthodox Church and the Ukrainian Autocephalous Orthodox Church", *Harvard Ukrainian Studies*, 1, 1979-80, pp. 92-111.

D. Brandenberger, *National Bolshevism*, Cambridge, Mass. 2002.

Budivnyctvo Radjans'koï Ukraïny [*The Construction of Soviet Ukraine*], Charkiv 1928.

K. Brown, *A Biography of no Place. From Ethnic Borderland to Soviet Heartland*, Cambridge, Mass. 2003.

O. Chlevnjuk, *Stalin-Kaganovič. Perepiska* [*Stalin-Kaganovič. Correspondence*], Moscow 2001.

N.B. Dirks, *Foreword* to Bernard S. Cohen, *Colonialism and Its Forms of Knowledge: The British in India*, Princeton 1996.

Korotki pidsumky perepysu naselennja Ukraïny 17 hrudnja roku 1926, Charkiv.

S. Kosior, *Itogi i bližajšie zadači provedenija nacional'noj politiki na Ukraine* [*Results and Immediate Tasks of the National Policy in Ukraine*], Moscow 1933.

Kul'turne budivnyctvo, I, Zbirka postanov pro ukraïnizaciju [*The Culture's Construction. Collection of Resolutions on Ukainization*], Cherson 1929.

M. Kundera, "The Tragedy of Central Europe", *The New York Review of Books*, 31, 7, 1984, pp. 33-38.

F. Hirsch, "Race without the Practice of Racial Politics", *Slavic Rewiev*, 1, 2002, pp. 30-43.

F. Hirsch, *Empire of Nations. Ethnographic Knowledge and the Making of the Soviet Union*, Ithaca, NY 2005.

V. Holubnychy, *Selected Works*, Edmonton 1982.

D. Lebed', "Nekotorye voprosy partijnogo s"ezda", ["Some Questions of the Party Congress"], *Kommunist*, March 17, 1923.

V. Lenin, *Lenin pro Ukraïnu* [*Lenin on Ukraine*], vol. II, Kyïv 1959.

G.O. Liber, *Soviet Nationality Policy, Urban Growth, and Identity Change in the Ukrainian SSR 1923-1934*, Cambridge 1992.

P. Ljubčenko, "Pro «derusyfikaciju» ta «polorusiv»" ["On «de-Russification» and the «Cumans»"], *Komunist*, June 28, 1933.

J. Mace, *Communism and the Dilemmas of National Liberation. National Communism in Soviet Ukraine, 1918-1933*, Cambridge, Mass. 1983.

I. Majstrenko, *Istorija moho pokolinnja* [*History of My Generation*], Edmonton 1985.

T. Martin, *The Affirmative Action Empire. Nations and Nationalism in the Soviet Union, 1923-1939*, Ithaca and London 2001.

Mis'ki selyšča USSR. Zbirnyk stat.-ekonomičnych vidomostej [*Urban Settlements in USSR. Collection of Stat.-economical data*] Charkiv 1929.

G. Perri, *Stato d'eccezione. L'internamento dei civili nel secondo conflitto mondiale in Gran Bretagna, Francia, Usa e Italia. Uno studio comparato*, Rome 2013.

S. Plokhy, *Unmaking Imperial Russia. Mykhailo Hrushevsky and the Wrtiting of Ukrainian History*, Toronto, Buffalo, London 2005.

O. Popov, "Narodne hospodarstvo Ukraïny ta Radjans'kyj Sojuz" ["The National Economy of Ukraine and Soviet Union"], *Žyttja j revoljucija*, 8, 1925, pp. 59-67.

J. Radziejowski, *The Communist Party of Western Ukraine. 1919-1929*, Edmonton 1983.

M. Ravič-Čerkasskij, *Istorija kommunističeskoj Partii (b-ov) Ukrainy* [*History of the Communist Party (Bolshevik) of Ukraine*], Charkiv 1923.

M. Skrypnyk, "Z pryvodu ekonomičnoï platformy nacionalizmu" ["Regarding the Nationalism's Economic Platform"], *Bil'šovyk Ukraïny*, 6, 1928, pp. 45-50.

M. Skrypnyk, *Do teoriï borot'by dvoch kul'tur* [*On the Theory of the Struggle between Two Cultures*], Charkiv 1928.

M. Skrypnyk, *Perebudovnymy šljachamy* [*On the adjustment paths*], in L. Masenko (ed.), *Ukraïns'ka mova u XX storičči* [*The Ukrainian Language in the Twentieth Century*], Kyïv 2005, pp. 38-91.

M. Skrypnyk, *Statti i promovy z nacional'noho pytannja* [*Articles and Speeches on the National Question*], Munich 1974.

Y. Slezkine, "The USSR as a Communal Apartment, or How Socialist State Promoted Ethnic Particularism", *Slavic Review*, 2, 1994, pp. 414-452.

I. Stalin, *Marksizm i nacional'no-kolonial'nyj vopros* [*Marxism and the National-Colonial Problem*], Moscow 1934.

I. Stalin, *Sočinenija* [*Works*], vol. 13, Moscow 1953.

O. Subtelny, *Ukraine. A History*, Toronto, Buffalo, London 2102.

R. Szporluk, "Kiev as the Ukraine's primate city", *Harvard Ukrainian Studies,* 3-4, 1979-1980, pp. 843-849.

Tajny nacional'noj politiki CK RKP: «Četvërtoe soveščanie CK RKP s otvetstvennymi rabotnikami nacional'nych respublik i oblastej v g. Moskve 9-12 ijunja 1923 g.». Stenografičeskij Otčët [*The Secrets of the National Policy of the Central Committee of the RKP: «Forth Meeting of the Central Committee of the RKP with the Responsible Workers of Republics and Regions, in Moscow on 9-12 June 1923». Stenographic Records*], Moscow 1992.

M. Volobujev, "Proty ekonomičnoï platformy nacionalizmu (Do krytyky volobujevščyny)" ["Against the Economic Platform of Nationalism (Toward a Critique of the Volubejsm)"], *Bil'šovyk Ukraïny* 1930, 5-6, pp. 59-69; 7, pp. 28-40.

M. Volobujev, "Do problemy ukraïns'koï ekonomiky" ["The Problem of the Ukrainian Economy"], in *Dokumenty ukraïns'koho komunizmu* [*Documents of the Ukrainian Communism*], New York 1962, pp. 132-250.

V. Vynnyčenko, *Vidrodžennja naciï* [*The Rebirth of the Nation*], vol. III, Kyïv and Vienna 1920.

E.D. Weitz, "Racial Politics without The Concept of Race: Reevaluating Soviet Ethnic and National Purges", *Slavic Rewiev* 1, 2002, pp. 1-29.

PERIODICALS

Bol'ševik
Pravda
Visti VUCVK (Bulletin of the Central Committee of the Communist Party of Ukraine)

Published Sources

Odynadcjatyj z"izd KP(b)U. Stenohrafičnyj zvit [*Eleventh Congress of the CP(Bolshevik)U. Stenographic Records*], Charkiv 1930.

Vtoraja sessija CIK SSSR 3 sozyva, 15-25 apr. 1926. Stenografič. Otčët [*The Second Session of the Centrale Executive Committee of the USSR, 3th Convocation, 15-25 April. 1926. Stenogr. Records*], Moscow 1926.

XII z"izd KP(b)U. Stenohrafičnyj zvit [*Twelfth Congress of the CP(Bolshevik)U. Stenographic Records*], Kyïv-Charkiv 1934.

XVI s"ezd vsesojuznoj kommunističeskoj partii VKP/b. Stenografičeskij otčët [*Sixteenth Congress of the Pansovietic Communist Party PCP/Bolshevik. Stenographic Records*], Moscow 1930.

XVII s"ezd vsesojuznoj kommunističeskoj partii/b. 26 janvarja-10 fevralja 1934 g. Stenografičeskij otčët [*Seventeenth Congress of the Pansovietic Communist Party/Bolshevik. 26 January-10 Feburary 1934*], Moscow 1934.

Archives

CSASBPGU - Central State Archives of Supreme Bodies of Power and Government of Ukraine (Central'nyj deržavnyj archiv vyščych orhaniv ta upravlinnja Ukraïny)

CSAPOU - Central State Archive of Public Organizations of Ukraine (Central'nyj deržavnyj archiv hromads'kych Ob"jednan' Ukraïny)

RSASPH - Russian State Archive of Socio-Political History (Rossijskij gosudarstvennyj archiv social'no-političeskoj istorii),

SARF - State Archive of the Russian Federation (Gosudarstvennyj archiv Rossijskoj Federacii).

Index

Introduction 5

1. Latin Ukraine 13

2. Print Culture in Early Modern Ukraine 19

3. The Prologue to the *Narcissus* of Hryhorij Skovoroda:
A Synthesis of the Modern Ukrainian Culture 35

4. Poland in the Humanistic Historiosophy of Taras Ševčenko 55

5. Cross Identity of a Metaphysician of Sensuality:
Jarosław Iwaszkiewicz 69

6. Independence: Literature, Historiography and Memory
of the Ukrainian National Republic (1917-1921) 83

7. Between Literature and Cinema: *Shadows of Forgotten Ancestors* 99

Appendix
Korenizacija as an ambiguous strategy of legitimization
of Soviet power in Ukraine (1923-1933) 115

Lightning Source UK Ltd.
Milton Keynes UK
UKHW011059050822
406887UK00003B/224